The Economist

INFREQUENTLY ASKED QUESTIONS

THE ECONOMIST IN ASSOCIATION WITH
PROFILE BOOKS LTD

Published by Profile Books Ltd
58A Hatton Garden, London EC1N 8LX

Copyright © The Economist Newspaper Ltd, 2001

"Infrequently asked questions" was written by Emily Bobrow,
Sarah Dallas, Kate Galbraith, Anthony Gottlieb, Lane Greene,
Jessica Harbour, David Newman, Barney Southin,
Shehnaz Suterwalla and Dawn Webster

All rights reserved. Without limiting the rights under copyright
reserved above, no part of this publication may be reproduced,
stored in or introduced into a retrieval system, or transmitted, in any
form or by any means (electronic, mechanical, photocopying,
recording or otherwise), without the prior written permission of
both the copyright owner and the publisher of this book.

The greatest care has been taken in compiling this book.
However, no responsibility can be accepted by the publishers or
compilers for the accuracy of the information presented.

Designed and typeset in EcoType by MacGuru
info@macguru.org.uk

Printed in Great Britain by
Bookmarque Ltd, Croydon, Surrey

A CIP catalogue record for this book is available
from the British Library

ISBN 1 86197 415 9

Introduction

Unless you are far too well-informed already, and cursed with an unselective memory, you could learn a great deal about world affairs, business, science and the arts from this book. A great deal of trivia, that is. For the facts it contains, though they may often be oddly memorable, mildly fascinating or bizarre, rarely matter. The book is designed for entertainment. Yet it does have a philosophical message.

The message is that truth is indeed often stranger than fiction, but in unpredictable ways. That is why these questions are so difficult. The compilers of the questions, each of which is based on an article from *The Economist*, have worked hard to throw readers off the scent. If you get more than half the answers right, you are doing well. If you laugh at the made-up answers as much as at the true ones, we shall be satisfied.

These puzzles are a selection from "Infrequently asked questions", Economist.com's current-affairs quiz. A new question is added every working day, at:

www.economist.com/diversions/quiz

To read the full articles on which the questions in this book are based, please go to:

www.economist.com/quizbook

QUESTIONS

1   Most Hollywood stars are best remembered for their bodies rather than their brains. Why was Hedy Lamarr an exception?

a   She co-led the Motion Picture Association of America's opposition to the Hollywood blacklist between 1947 and 1951
b   She wrote a series of critically acclaimed novellas under the name of Eve Kisser
c   She attained a doctorate in philosophy from the University of Vienna, at the age of 56
d   She invented a military communications technology, a refinement of which can now be found in mobile phones

2   America's CIA has projected that by 2015 the country is:

a   "Likely" to face a missile threat from North Korea, and that such a threat is "highly unlikely" from Libya and "impossible" from the Sudan
b   "Certain" to face a missile threat from North Korea, but such a threat is only "possible" from Britain and "unlikely" from Afghanistan
c   "Likely" to face a missile threat from North Korea, and that such a threat is "probable" from Iran and "possible" from Iraq
d   "Certain" to face a missile threat from North Korea, but such a threat is merely "feasible" from Iraq and "highly unlikely" from Belgium

ANSWERS

1 **(d) She invented a military communications technology, a refinement of which can now be found in mobile phones**

Miss Lamarr developed the idea in collaboration with George Antheil, a composer she met in 1940 at a party in Hollywood. Applying their knowledge of musical harmony they devised a technology for military communications. In 1942 they were granted an American patent for the invention. The army was not interested, the patent eventually expired and the couple never profited. Today, though, a development of the invention, known as spread-spectrum technology, is being used in a wide range of electronic products, including mobile phones. Engineers reckon the concept is, so to speak, just beautiful.

Hedy Lamarr, *The Economist*, January 29th 2000

2 **(c) "Likely" to face a missile threat from North Korea, and that such a threat is "probable" from Iran and "possible" from Iraq**

Made known to the American public in the weeks before the presidential election, the predictions quickly became a mainstay in the case for an American anti-missile defence programme. The timetable is based on estimates that North Korea could develop a missile capable of hitting the United States in five years' time. Indeed, North Korea's launch in August 1998 of a three-stage rocket shocked the world. Once again, western experts had underestimated the ballistic missile technology of anti-American regimes. But would such rockets ever be fired against the United States? It would seem suicidal. It is possible, nonetheless, to imagine a regional crisis in which America's freedom to support local allies would be hampered by the knowledge that its territory could, however hypothetically, be attacked with missiles.

A shield in space, *The Economist*, June 3rd 2000

QUESTIONS

3 **As the Gore campaign underlined, George W. Bush's environmental record as governor of Texas was less than perfect. For example:**

a One in every seven Texas cattle has been treated for a respiratory disease caused by air pollution
b Were Texas a country in its own right, it would be the world's seventh-biggest national emitter of carbon dioxide
c Thanks to overactive immune systems irritated by smog, most of Houston's cats are allergic to people
d The Rio Grande and Colorado rivers now contain a volume of industrial waste equivalent to that dumped in the North Sea between 1960 and 1990

4 **Kwaito, a derivative of American gangsta rap, has become the favourite dance music of young, black South Africans. Legend has it that Kwaito began in the early 1990s when:**

a A township disc jockey spun a dance track at the wrong speed
b Teenagers discovered they could build record-players from discarded car parts
c Rapper Ice-T played a sell-out concert in Soweto in 1991
d A pirate radio station held a competition for people who could sing backwards

ANSWERS

3 (b) Were Texas a country in its own right, it would be the world's seventh-biggest national emitter of carbon dioxide

Are things in Texas really that bad? And was George W. Bush's stretch as governor to blame? To the first question, the answer is undoubtedly yes. As the heart of America's petrochemical and oil-refining industries, Texas puts more chemicals into the air than any other state, and by most rankings is the state with the worst toxin level in the atmosphere. But, as Bush defenders are quick to point out, Texas's environmental woes are nothing new. The latest data from the NAFTA Environmental Commission show that Texas's toxic release levels actually declined by 15% from 1995 to 1997, suggesting that cows and cats can now breathe more easily.

The Lone Smog State, *The Economist*, July 22nd 2000

4 (a) A township disc jockey spun a dance track at the wrong speed

Legend has it that the crowd loved the miscue. Soon, several DJs were playing British house music and American rap deliberately slowly. Some added their own lyrics. The new sound inspired new dances: the sexy "butterfly", the hip-twisting twaladza. Kwaito swiftly became the dance music for black South Africans. Many black South Africans over 30, who grew up on protest songs, found kwaito's apolitical materialism disturbing. Parents were upset to see their children idolising what appeared to be bellowing hoodlums. But kwaito mellowed. Perhaps because life for the average young black South African is much more dangerous than it is for the average young black American, songs glorifying murder do not sell well.

One way to get rich in Soweto, *The Economist*, March 4th 2000

QUESTIONS

5 Japanese animation is slowly gaining acceptance in the West. The film "Princess Mononoke", which opened to rave reviews in America, tells the story of:

a A schoolgirl's obsessive search through Tokyo's underworld for her missing father
b A medieval people's epic battle with the forces of nature
c An inept businessman's comic attempts to woo a girl working at a noodle bar
d A telepathic monkey's journey to the edge of the galaxy

6 In its early days, taxation did not always involve money. For example:

a During the reign of Ptolemy I, Egyptian farmers paid a tax of one pomegranate for the right to plough one furrow
b The Jivaro tribesmen of the Amazon paid their taxes with shrunken heads
c After the Black Death, surviving villagers from Dunsten in Norfolk were allowed to pay their taxes with jewellery taken from the dead
d Japanese fishermen once paid their imperial taxes with shipments of live octopuses

ANSWERS

5 (b) A medieval people's epic battle with the forces of nature

For all the critical acclaim, the American earnings of "Princess Mononoke" were less than spectacular, particularly when considering that the film crossed the Pacific as the all-time champion of Japan's domestic box office. Families, expecting typical Disney fare, may well have been shocked by the film's mature themes. Even by the more macabre standards of the *anime* genre, "Mononoke" tends toward the dark and disturbing, with a generous share of violence, death and even sexuality, as well as a conclusion that seemingly resolves nothing. The increasingly stunning animation emerging from the United States (in films like "A Bug's Life" and "Toy Story 2") is, quite literally, child's play alongside the full-length animated films that have been pouring out of Japan since the early 1980s.

Toy stories for grown-ups, *The Economist*, February 26th 2000

6 (b) The Jivaro tribesmen of the Amazon paid their taxes with shrunken heads

Prostitution may be the oldest profession, but tax collection was surely not far behind. The Bible records that Jesus offered his views on a tax matter, and converted a prominent taxman. In its early days taxation did not always involve handing over money. The ancient Chinese paid with pressed tea. And as a price of citizenship, ancient Greeks and Romans could be called on to serve as soldiers, and even had to supply their own weapons. Then there are the Jivaro tribesmen in the Amazon region, who stumped up shrunken heads in what is surely the most literal-minded interpretation of, ahem, the death tax.

A brief history of tax, *The Economist*, January 29th 2000

QUESTIONS

7 **In February 2000, America's Aerospace Corporation sent two miniature satellites into orbit. Approximately how big was each "picosatellite"?**

a The size of a modern golf ball
b Slightly larger than a fresh pineapple
c The size of a packet of Marlboro Menthol Lights
d Slightly smaller than a Hitachi portable television

8 **According to some anthropologists, St Valentine's day originated in lusty fertility rituals such as the Roman festival of Lupercalia. What happened at Lupercalia?**

a Young women stripped naked, rolled in honey, and offered their bodies to the god Lupercus
b Athletes competed for the right to present their lovers with a bunch of flowers
c Amorous couples exchanged gifts of raw meat, vine leaves and oysters
d Men, clad in goatskins, flagellated the local female population

ANSWERS

7 (c) The size of a packet of Marlboro Menthol Lights

Admittedly, these pioneering picosatellites cannot do much – but then, neither could *Sputnik*. Like that vehicle, they are there to prove a principle. They will use their radio transmitters to exchange data with each other, and with a third picosat on the ground. They will also test an array of components constructed using micro-electro-mechanical systems (MEMS) technology. This borrows fabrication techniques from the semiconductor industry to carve tiny mechanical devices out of silicon. Although such satellites are small and (at least currently) incapable, that has not stopped their proponents from thinking big – because several small satellites may often be preferable to a single, large one, costing less to launch and allowing defects to be remedied piecemeal.

Small is beautiful, *The Economist*, February 5th 2000

8 (d) Men, clad in goatskins, flagellated the local female population

Exchanging gifts on St Valentine's day is as old as the feast itself, which was celebrated in the market-square economies of the Middle Ages. But the festivity has more to do with the time of year than with Saint Valentine, of whom there were at least three, two of whom were beheaded in the third century. All are venerated on February 14th, but none seems to have had anything to do with love. St Valentine's day is more appropriately associated with the coupling of birds and the return of spring, thanks mainly to Chaucer's "Parliament of Fowls" (1382), one of the first valentine poems in English. Some anthropologists link the feast to end-of-winter rituals such as the Roman Lupercalia, when men clad in goatskins went around flagellating all the women in sight in order to make them fertile.

Of love and dividends, *The Economist*, February 12th 2000

QUESTIONS

9 Americans are spending more money than ever on bodily "augmentations". Which one of the following is true?

a Eight percent of people who undergo such augmentations work in the financial-services sector
b Between 1992 and 1998 the number of cosmetic surgical procedures grew almost as quickly as the Dow
c The average breast augmentation costs less than a ten-year subscription to *The Economist* print edition
d In 1997 more money was spent on chemical peels than was traded on the Nasdaq on June 15th of the same year

10 Samuel Beckett nurtured ambitions to make it in films. This led him to collaborate with:

a Charlie Chaplin, who produced several films with Mr Beckett while in voluntary exile in Switzerland
b Marilyn Monroe; after several years' correspondence, Mr Beckett wrote her a screenplay, which he destroyed after her death
c Buster Keaton; Mr Beckett wrote "Film", Mr Keaton's last silent movie
d Jean-Luc Godard, who planned to film "Waiting for Godot", but quarrelled with Mr Beckett and made "Breathless" instead

ANSWERS

9 (b) Between 1992 and 1998 the number of cosmetic surgical procedures grew almost as quickly as the Dow

One way to test the buoyancy of Nasdaq is to observe the blouses and trousers of America. While their investment accounts were swelling, Americans were laying out more money than ever for tucks, lifts, implants, peels, injections and assorted "augmentations". The number of cosmetic surgical procedures was growing almost as quickly as the Dow – from 413,000 in 1992 to over 1m in 1998. The until-recently booming stockmarket is not the only reason for all this nipping and tucking. Another factor is the demographic bulge. The baby-boomers are reaching the age where assorted body parts are feeling (and worse, showing) the effects of time and gravity. Ironically, given the complaints about the bubble economy, the most common body upgrade is liposuction.

Putting a brave face on Nasdaq, *The Economist*, July 15th 2000

10 (c) Buster Keaton; Mr Beckett wrote "Film", Mr Keaton's last silent movie

In 1936 Samuel Beckett, arguably Ireland's greatest playwright, wrote to Sergei Eisenstein, arguably Russia's greatest film maker, to ask if he could train with the Moscow State Institute of Cinematography. This unlikely alliance came to nothing, but Beckett's interest in film persisted, notably in his collaboration with Buster Keaton on "Film" (Keaton's last silent movie). Radio and television plays such as "All that Fall" and "Eh Joe" show that Beckett was keen to explore different dramatic media. Nevertheless, he declined many offers to make films from his plays, including requests from such eminent directors as Ingmar Bergman. Recent film versions of Beckett plays have been disappointing; viewers can only dream of what a Beckett screenplay for Marilyn Monroe or Jean-Luc Godard might have been.

Summer of Sam, *The Economist*, June 2nd 2001

QUESTIONS

11 A study by three economists in July 2000 valued the overall contribution of financial analysts as:

a   Modest at best
b   Grossly undervalued, especially by journalists
c   Fundamental to successful investment, at least in developed countries
d   A waste of time and money

12 According to the "Yale Dictionary of Quotations", the earliest known published use of the word "software" occurred in:

a   An after-dinner speech given by Marshall McLuhan to Harvard University's cheerleaders
b   A book entitled "Binary Computing", written by a statistician, Joseph Lansing
c   An article published in *American Mathematical Monthly* in 1958
d   A 1947 edition of the racy magazine "Swell Chicks and Big, Swinging Dicks"

ANSWERS

11 (a) Modest at best

The study looked at the returns earned by investors in American shares, and calculated how much of the differences in returns could be predicted from traditional financial indicators based on company accounts. They then repeated this analysis adding as an extra crystal ball analysts' profit forecasts. At first, the economists found the profit forecasts very helpful in predicting differences in share returns. However, they then looked at whether analysts were still useful if investors also relied on past changes in share prices to guide their expectations. It turned out they were not much help. Indeed, the economists reckon that analysts making forecasts mostly took their lead from changes in market values. As share prices rose (or fell), the analysts raised (or lowered) their profits forecasts. Share analysts: underperforming; sell.

Downgraded, *The Economist*, July 22nd 2000

12 (c) An article published in *American Mathematical Monthly* in 1958

A Princeton mathematician, John Tukey, long credited with whittling "binary digit" down to "bit", was also, it now seems, the first to employ "software" in its modern use. His 1958 article in *American Mathematical Monthly* fashioned the term as a shortcut for "the carefully planned interpretive routines, compilers, and other aspects of automative programming". But the OED could yet have the last word on "software". A member of the OED staff has uncovered an example of the word dating back to 1850, though in a rather different context. At that time, "soft-ware" and "hard-ware" were terms used by rubbish-tip pickers to distinguish compost from non-biodegradable matter. So a Victorian would have been baffled by the modern use of the term. Garbage in, garbage out, as computer programmers like to say.

How software got its name, *The Economist*, June 3rd 2000

QUESTIONS

13 Sometimes the early career of a country's leader matches his personality. For example:

a Yugoslavia's ex-president Slobodan Milosevic spent a year in his late 20s serving as a state prison guard in Nis, a city in southern Serbia
b Kenya's president Daniel arap Moi, a man obsessed with his own image, rose from oblivion by selling mirrors for a British company's Nairobi branch
c Belarus's president Alexander Lukashenka, adept at ruffling western feathers, managed a state chicken farm during his younger days
d While at Oxford, Britain's prime minister Tony Blair earned pocket money by bartending at a pub called the Third Wave

14 Europeans like to stereotype other Europeans. Mediterraneans consider northerners to be tall, fat, boozy and depressed single parents. Northerners say that their southern cousins are stumpy, chain-smokers with maniacal driving habits. Which of the following is true?

a Germans knock back 30% more alcohol each year than the temperate Dutch, most of it on Fridays
b French married couples are 20% more likely to stay together than Finnish couples and have more sex
c Austrians outweigh the Portuguese by an average of 9kg
d In Finland there are ten psychiatrists for every 1,000 people (compared with five per 1,000 in France)

ANSWERS

13 (c) Belarus's president Alexander Lukashenka, adept at ruffling western feathers, managed a state chicken farm during his younger days

Alexander Lukashenka, the former collective farm manager, is a cunning cynic with an alarming range of populist skills which helped him win office in a free presidential election. Since then he has destroyed his legitimacy in every way available. He has rewritten the constitution, extended his term, sacked parliament, appointed a new constitutional court, muzzled the media, suppressed opposition movements, given free rein to an unreformed (and unrenamed) KGB, and reimposed central planning across the economy. He has made himself, in effect, an elected dictator, and condemned his country to poverty and misery in the process. So Belarus may be the only country in the whole of the ex-communist zone consciously to head back east, and even to want to reunite with Russia.

Ten years since the wall fell, *The Economist*, November 6th 1999

14 (c) Austrians outweigh the Portuguese by an average of 9kg

According to Eurostat, the EU's statistics office, there is a good deal of truth behind the stereotypes, especially when it comes to sizes and shapes. Northern Europeans tower over others, literally. The average young Dutchman, Europe's tallest chap, just ahead of his Danish and Swedish counterparts, stands nine centimetres ($3^1/_2$ inches) above his Spanish and Portuguese cousins, although even the latter have sprouted by eight centimetres in the past 40 years. As for booze, the Irish do quaff a fair bit, but their Gallic counterparts outdo them. Greeks raise their glasses less than most, but perhaps that is because the cigarette between their lips gets in the way: they smoke almost twice the EU average, and nearly five times as much as the Norwegians.

What a lot of sterEUtypes, *The Economist*, October 23rd 1999

15 Which of the following was a target of the British government in its July 2000 spending review?

a Increase England's badger and fox population by 300%, but decrease the amount of stoats by an eighth
b Reverse the long-term decline in the number of farmland birds by 2020 "as measured annually against underlying trends"
c Encourage the proliferation of flying beetles in wooded areas, with the exception of the New Forest and the Forest of Dean
d Re-introduce three packs of wolves to the Scottish Highlands, "dependent upon consumption of livestock"

16 In the summer of 2000 it seemed that America's mobile-phone industry might be lurching towards disaster because:

a The best frequencies for new voice and data services had already been snapped up by television stations, security-alarm firms and the military
b Japanese 3G mobile telephones were threatening to put American mobile-phone manufacturers out of business
c The Federal Communications Commission postponed the auction of the 700-megahertz band until 2004
d Wally Waveband, the Federal Communications Commission's mascot, had been ominously killed by a speeding dumpster at an Orlando conference in April

ANSWERS

15 **(b) Reverse the long-term decline in the number of farmland birds by 2020 "as measured annually against underlying trends"**

For now, the stoats can rest easy. But the idea of all this target-setting was that British government departments would have to deliver genuine, measurable improvements in public services. They were meant to be more precise and demanding than the relatively vague goals set in 1998. The government wanted to raise employment, cut the number of unemployed people and improve productivity. Quite exacting, but the Treasury added an all-purpose qualification: "taking into account the economic cycle". And government by targets has problems that go beyond its inherent tendency to absurdity. Targets can distort bureaucratic behaviour. Official efforts are directed to meeting a national number, rather than real needs on the ground.

Target mad, *The Economist*, July 29th 2000

16 **(a) The best frequencies for new voice and data services have already been snapped up by television stations, security-alarm firms and the military**

Compared with most European countries, America's airwaves are impossibly cluttered, thanks to the fact that the country was an early adopter of commercial wireless services of all sorts (early radio technology was far "leakier" than today's, and so had to use broader frequency bands to avoid interfering with other services). The sweetest band of all, that in the 700 megahertz range, where signals can travel easily through buildings, is occupied by UHF TV channels that are used by about 100 stations scattered around the country. Experts estimate that by 2005 the wireless services now in use or planned will require 350–460 megahertz of spectrum, two to three times what is currently available.

Battle of the airwaves, *The Economist*, July 29th 2000

QUESTIONS

17 George W. Bush appears to have inherited the verbal eccentricities of his maundering father. Which one of the following has not (yet) been uttered by "Dubya"?

a   Better education means lesser stupidity
b   We ought to make the pie higher
c   Will the highways on the Internet become more few?
d   I think anybody who doesn't think I'm smart enough to handle the job is underestimating

18 A study by Thomas Zentall of the University of Kentucky found that, like people, pigeons:

a   Need to consume more than twice their body-weight each month in order to stay healthy
b   Cannot differentiate the points of the compass if they are spun around on a swivel chair
c   Can be tricked into thinking that what they've worked hard for is actually better for them
d   Pick their noses

ANSWERS

17 (a) Better education means lesser stupidity

It is no crime not to go to the opera and to prefer "Cats" and the music of Van Morrison; having literary tastes that run the gamut from A (spy novels) to B (detective stories) is no disqualification either. But to boast – as Mr Bush did – that he doesn't waste his time reading 500-page policy tomes is somewhat different: that suggests a disengagement from the details of public policy and even a lack of intellectual curiosity that is at least relevant to his job application. He reads his speeches as if his voice and his brain were operating independently of one another. Like his father, he pauses in the wrong places and mangles phrases (exemplary comes out as exemplarary, tactical nuclear weapons as tacular weapons). Maybe we are "misunderestimating" him, but the stumbles are hardly the way to keep the world from wondering.

Preparing America for compassionate conservatism, *The Economist*, July 29th 2000

18 (c) Can be tricked into thinking that what they've worked hard for is actually better for them

Dr Zentall trained a small band of pigeons to tap two different buttons if they wanted a snack. The pigeons had to tap the red button only once to be rewarded; the green button meant a tiresome 20 pecks before the grain was delivered. The pigeons soon learnt the difference. But which button would they pick if free to choose? Classical theory suggests that the pigeon should not really care: both buttons preceded the same reward. If anything, a clever pigeon would associate the red button with less work. Yet the pigeons opted for the green button twice as often as the red one. The effort seemed, according to Dr Zentall, to make the grain more valuable. The phrase "bird-brained" somehow comes winging to mind.

Puritanical pigeons, *The Economist*, August 5th 2000

QUESTIONS

19 India's film industry is growing up. For example:

a   18 Hindi films grossed more than £25m in 2000, including "Rupee Whoopee" and "I Left my Heart in Hydrabad"
b   India makes more films than the United States
c   In Bollywood, home of the Hindi movie industry, there are 300 actors for each movie camera
d   The Indian government is constructing two new power stations, solely to meet the growing electricity needs of Bollywood's film studios

20 Despite the European Union's best efforts, cannabis is flowing from Morocco into Europe in vast quantities. Each year:

a   Morocco's cannabis crop brings in about $4 billion
b   King Mohammed enjoys a ceremonial spliff on the slopes of Mount Toubkal, North Africa's "highest" peak
c   Moroccan traffickers attempt to smuggle 2,000 tonnes of hashish past European customs officers
d   Another 3,000 hectares of barren land is turned over to Morocco's cannabis growers

ANSWERS

19 (b) **India makes more films than the United States**

Some 700 films are made in India each year, more than in any other country. This leads optimists to view India as a prospective low-cost producer for the global movie industry. Controlled by a few powerful movie producers – often tycoons or former actors – the industry is largely self-financed, but at a high cost. (A few years ago, for instance, foreign investors poured money into a promising entertainment venture linked to Amitabh Bachchan, Bollywood's biggest star. It was struggling within months, and eventually went bust.) Private finance, some of it from underworld sources, is secured at usurious rates. Small wonder that only a fifth of all movies make a profit. And big investors remain wary of Bollywood's reputation for murky dealings and cost overruns.

Growing up, *The Economist*, August 12th 2000

20 (c) **Moroccan traffickers attempt to smuggle 2,000 tonnes of hashish past European customs officers**

Morocco is the world's largest hashish exporter and the supplier of more than 70% of the EU's intake. Its cannabis crop is estimated to earn it over $2 billion a year, the great bulk of the money going to the traffickers – and the officials they bribe. Moreover, the drug trade provides an income for one of Morocco's poorest and most unruly regions, the Rif mountains. In 1999, farmers gave King Mohammed a rapturous welcome when he made a trip through the cannabis heartlands of Ketama, the first monarch to visit this sweet-perfumed land in 40 years. Though he stopped short of his grandfather's custom of accepting a spliff, the king maintains a discreet silence on his kingdom's leading hard-currency spinner.

Want some weed?, *The Economist*, August 19th 2000

QUESTIONS

21 **Jack Ma, a passionate translator and xenophile, aimed to build China's first global e-commerce firm. Yet the inspiration for his grandiose scheme came in less than auspicious circumstances:**

a   He was being held captive by a gun-toting crook in a Malibu beach house, after a business deal had gone disastrously wrong
b   He was lying in a Shanghai hospital bed, having being beaten-up by a gang of irate schoolboys
c   He was trapped in the hold of a cargo ship on its way to Panama
d   He was delivering pizzas in the San Francisco hills, using a motorcycle with no brakes

22 **What was the idea behind a paper by two members of the University of Michigan Business School entitled "Is Sound Just Noise?"**

a   The acoustical qualities of the world's trading floors play an under-appreciated role in governing the behaviour of financial markets
b   Noisy air-conditioning distracts employees, leading to a decrease in office-wide productivity
c   Listening to repetitive music, such as German "techno", can boost office work rates in accordance with the music's bpm (beats-per-minute)
d   Noisy traders create a "buzz" in the pit before the information hits the market

ANSWERS

21 **(a) He was being held captive by a gun-toting crook in a Malibu beach house, after a business deal had gone disastrously wrong**

Dispatched to Malibu to resolve a business dispute with an American businessman, the slight, owlish Mr Ma soon twigged that the company he was investigating did not exist, that his host was a crook, and that he himself was in serious danger. After Mr Ma rebuffed offers of bribery, the American locked him in the beach house. A frightened Mr Ma, who had recently heard about the Internet, desperately suggested that the two try their luck at "doing business" together in China. His captor eventually agreed and set him free. It was only after he fled to Seattle that Mr Ma surfed the Internet for the first time. So inspired was he that, back in China, he really did start a dotcom, only without gangster backing.

The Jack who would be king, *The Economist*, August 26th 2000

22 **(d) Noisy traders create a "buzz" in the pit just before the information hits the market**

The paper is based on a simple premise: anxious market makers shout a lot when they think the cost of executing trades will soon rise, thus a "buzz" presages shifts in the market. When the need to trade is less urgent, floor traders make do with simple hand signals, which require less energy and are less likely to alert their competitors. The claim is supported by other studies showing that trading tends to migrate to open-outcry systems at times of extreme volatility. And the business world has also embraced the idea. A software company founded by two former traders, uses recorded voices to simulate the floor. By giving electronic traders an idea of what their market would sound like, the system claims to improve response time.

The sound and the fury, *The Economist*, August 26th 2000

QUESTIONS

23 **What would you find in *il Gabinetto segreto* ("the secret room"), which in the spring of 2000 opened its doors to the Neapolitan public for the first time since 1971?**

a   A collection of antique flick-knives inscribed with Mafia code-words
b   The decapitated remains of St Januarius, the patron saint of Naples
c   Various "obscene objects" from the ruins of Pompeii and Herculaneum, including a lamp depicting a gladiator locked in combat with his monstrous phallus
d   Enrico Caruso's soiled underwear

24 **According to a study by Lesley-Anne King of the University of Oxford, aggression among commercially reared chickens can be tempered by:**

a   Putting them in pens with larger, territorial farm animals such as pigs and goats
b   Feeding them large quantities of St John's wort
c   Introducing bales of wood-shavings into their pens
d   Taking the troublemakers to one side and beating them in front of other chickens

ANSWERS

23 (c) Various "obscene objects" from the ruins of Pompeii and Herculaneum, including a lamp depicting a gladiator locked in combat with his monstrous phallus

Ovid and Martial, among others, always taught that the Romans, even if coarser than the Greeks, knew a lot about the *Ars amatoria*. The aura of scandal which has surrounded for so long these illustrations of how they performed will now perhaps diminish. It is ironic, as the museum's director explained recently while guiding visitors around the *Gabinetto*, that over the centuries most European courts, when embarrassed by objects they considered obscene in their collections, would consign them to Naples. To them, the *Gabinetto* was evidently considered a depository of pornography. Most of the museums in the world have their own secret rooms, probably even the Vatican. Perhaps it is time to open all the doors. Naples is setting an example.

Porn from Pompeii, *The Economist*, April 8th 2000

24 (c) Introducing bales of wood-shavings into their pens

In the control pens – without the bales – the birds spent 7% of their time drinking and 1% attacking others. Moreover, they pecked repeatedly at the air, which is also considered unhealthy behaviour. Those in the enriched environment, however, drank for half as long, and their aggressive head-pecking was all but eliminated. Instead, they spent far more of their time – up to a third – pecking at the inanimate objects in the pens. This suggests that bales could diminish aggression, reduce injuries, and mitigate respiratory problems. It might even improve productivity, because a happy chicken is a productive chicken.

How to deal with chicken-rage, *The Economist*, April 29th 2000

QUESTIONS

25 Between the ages of 13 and 72, Douglas Fairbanks, junior, acted in 79 forgettable films. Yet he achieved fame by other means. How?

a   By opening a chain of California steakhouses where meat was served with replica swords from his father's popular Zorro films
b   He was good company to royalty and Hollywood celebrities, entertaining Queen Elizabeth, among others, at his house in London
c   In the summer of 1949 Mr Fairbanks broke the American water-skiing speed record on Lake Walker
d   He won notoriety as a daring photographer in the Korean war

26 Work published by Richard Marlar, a pathologist at the University of Colorado Medical School, has leant weight to the theory that:

a   Ancient Americans occasionally ate one another
b   Weightlessness permanently damages astronauts' ability to balance
c   In some parts of Africa, AIDS is transmitted by vampire bats
d   It is physiologically impossible to sneeze with your eyes open

ANSWERS

25 (b) He was good company to royalty and Hollywood celebrities, entertaining Queen Elizabeth, among others, at his house in London

What Douglas Fairbanks excelled at was being famous. Attaining durable fame is a tricky feat, and Mr Fairbanks worked hard at it. Being good-looking helped. He flattered Britain by being excessively fond of it, and for many years had a splendid house in London. Queen Elizabeth, who had made him a knight for fostering Anglo-American relations, sometimes came to dinner. The queen is easily bored at dinner parties, but Mr Fairbanks always kept her interested with his stories. His films may have been duds, but he had known Garbo, Hepburn and Dietrich and all the others in Hollywood's classic era. He was good company, and not just to queens, but to everyone who knew him. This was his real métier as an entertainer.

Douglas Fairbanks, junior, *The Economist*, May 13th 2000

26 (a) Ancient Americans occasionally ate one another

Given the current climate of political correctness, the burden of proof for cannibalism has become heavier. Take the case of the Cowboy Wash, a dry stream bed in south-western Colorado, thought to be an ancient settlement of the Anasazi people. Butchery tools stained with human blood and the scattered, battered bones of seven people bearing the marks of those tools, had long suggested to scholars that something went very wrong here around 1150. Still, Cowboy Wash remained a source of debate until Dr Marlar detected the presence of human myoglobin, a protein that is found in muscle tissue, on fragments of a ceramic cooking pot and desiccated human faecal material.

Fine old cannibals, *The Economist*, September 9th 2000

27 Other than to attract foreign shipowners, why has landlocked Bolivia unfurled a flag of convenience?

a   The government has re-opened La Paz's naval academy, and wants its graduates to sail under the Bolivian flag
b   Tired of racing gunboats around Lake Titicaca, Bolivia's admirals are pressuring the government to buy a second-hand battleship
c   Paraguay and Suriname both launched flags of convenience, and Bolivia didn't want to be left out
d   Bolivia hopes to strengthen its claim to a piece of Pacific coastline that was lost in a 19th-century war

28 In Pakistan, 42% of men (aged 15 and above) and 71% of women are illiterate, according to the World Bank's *World Development Report 2000/2001*. Which of the following statements is also true?

a   South Korea, Argentina and Indonesia are emerging economies with virtually no illiteracy
b   In Niger, 98% of men cannot read or write
c   32% of Welshmen can read music but not sing
d   In Burkina Faso, 87% of women are illiterate

ANSWERS

27 (d) Bolivia hopes to strengthen its claim to a piece of Pacific coastline that was lost in a 19th-century war

Flags of convenience have always had a rather suspect air. Never more so, surely, than when they are run up by a country without a coastline. But for landlocked Bolivia, which lost its access to the Pacific in an 1884 war with Chile, the incongruity is exactly the point. Although it has no diplomatic relations with Chile, Bolivia continues to press its claim, holding regular talks with the Chilean government. With Chile unlikely to hand the land back, a corridor linking Bolivia to the sea appears to be the only realistic option. Technically, the flag will come under the auspices of the defence ministry. There, it will benefit from contact with the Bolivian navy, a Gilbert and Sullivan affair with admirals but no warships.

Bolivia waves the flag, *The Economist*, May 25th 2000

28 (d) In Burkina Faso, 87% of women are illiterate

Pakistan has the highest adult illiteracy rates of any big emerging economy, according to statistics published in the World Development Report. But illiteracy rates are higher than this in many extremely poor African countries: surpassing even Burkina Faso, shares of illiteracy in Niger are 78% for men and 93% for women. Pakistan stands out among emerging markets not only in the extent of illiteracy but also in the discrepancy between men and women. At the other extreme, South Korea, Argentina, Hungary and Russia (but not Indonesia) are emerging economies with virtually no illiteracy.

Illiteracy, *The Economist*, October 19th 2000

QUESTIONS

29 **There are no objective grounds for determining the price of a life, so academics and civil servants resort to asking people how much they would pay to avoid certain risks. The results of such research reveal that:**

a The French would much rather die in a road accident than an air crash
b Broadly speaking, the average British life is valued at £1m
c Broadly speaking, the average American life is valued at $300,000
d Most Russians say they would pay over $2m to avoid death by starvation

30 **In November 2000, Prince Rainier of Monaco attacked the French government in *Le Figaro*. The prince's uncharacteristic outburst was a response to the following:**

a In October a French parliamentary committee drew up a "black list" of Monte Carlo residents that it suspected of financial impropriety
b The French government threatened to end Monaco's special status as a tax haven, unless the principality introduced tighter financial regulations
c Rainier's daughter, Stephanie, had been held in police custody in Paris for three days, on colourful allegations that were later proved false
d Air France suspended flights to Monaco, claiming that the runway in Monte Carlo was too short

ANSWERS

29 **(b) Broadly speaking, the average British life is valued at £1m**

In Britain, the £1m figure varies little, from risk to risk. A life is a life, people reckon, however it is lost or saved. But the government, it seems, is not as rational as the people. Although deaths on the roads vastly outnumber deaths on the railways (by 3,423 to 33 in 1999) the railways command disproportionately high spending on safety. The advanced train protection system, already in place in some areas, would cost more than £2 billion to install nationally, implying a price on each life saved of more than £15m. The transport department's guidelines on road safety spending set a price of just over £1m per life. But a better indicator of investment in road safety, the one implied by local authorities' spending, is a miserly £100,000 per life.

The price of safety, *The Economist*, November 25th 2000

30 **(b) The French government threatened to end Monaco's special status as a tax haven, unless the principality introduced tighter financial regulations**

Monaco likes to portray itself as a secure haven for the well-behaved rich: per head GDP in 1999 was about $27,000 (about a third higher than in France) and there are more police for its size of population than almost anywhere else in the world. In other words, it hurts that successive French comments, from a parliamentary mission in June to reports in October from the ministers of finance and justice, should describe the principality as a sanctuary for tax dodgers, drug barons and money launderers. Unless Monaco cleans up its act, said the finance ministry in words all the more menacing for their vagueness, "the French government will propose to parliament legislative measures to put an end to such situations."

Could Monaco's luck run out?, *The Economist*, November 4th 2000

31 Who wrote this, and to whom? "Am at your service from here on. Godfather."

a "King of Cocaine" Roberto Suarez Gomez to then president of Bolivia, Luis Garcia Meza
b Frank Lloyd Wright to architecture critic Elizabeth Gordon
c Former British Labour minister Geoffrey Robinson to former Northern Ireland secretary Peter Mandelson
d J.D. Salinger to one of his mistresses

32 Why does a museum in Turkey have a plate of three shrivelled chickpeas on display?

a They were almost eaten by Mustafa Kemal Ataturk, the beloved "Father of the Turks"
b They offer clues about the diet of Ottoman army recruits at the end of the first world war
c They are the first successful products of a Turkish cloning experiment
d They are the national pea

ANSWERS

31 (b) Frank Lloyd Wright to architecture critic Elizabeth Gordon

Wright was then 87, the most famous architect in America and still working, but in the eyes of younger architects, especially those dazzled by the international style, a bit old-fashioned. Miss Gordon was flattered by her attention from Wright. She had had no training in architecture. After university she had first got a job writing advertising copy and had then taken up journalism. What Elizabeth Gordon had to offer Wright was a sharp pen and her magazine to use as a "propaganda tool". She set out to make him the symbol of all that was worthwhile in design. On three occasions, she devoted an entire issue of her magazine to his work.

Elizabeth Gordon, *The Economist*, September 30th 2000

32 (a) They were almost eaten by Mustafa Kemal Ataturk, the beloved "Father of the Turks"

When Ataturk died, in 1938, the government of the day commissioned a shrine to house not only his body but also his old cars, suits, golfing plus-fours, pyjamas, socks, unsmoked cigarettes, even his nail-clippers. In a souvenir shop you can buy Ataturk carpets, fridge magnets and CD-ROMS, not to mention a selection of snaps of a sun-kissed Ataturk in tight-fitting swimming trunks. A diverse stream of visitors shuffles by: giggling lovers, veiled housewives, impish children, conscripts, businessmen, pensioners, all united by their fascination with the most mundane details of Ataturk's daily life.

Ataturk's long shadow, *The Economist*, June 10th 2000

33 Which of the following outlandish proposals was among some 200 initiatives and referendums on America's electoral ballot in 2000?

a   Legalise medicinal marijuana in Alaska
b   Eliminate video gambling in South Carolina
c   Eliminate the ban on interracial marriage in Alabama
d   Legalise cocaine on death row in Texas

34 Which of these is a flaw in the way nations measure inflation?

a   The European Central Bank gives too little weight to pet costs, given that animal ownership is much more common in Europe than in the United States
b   The US index overestimates lower prices due to e-commerce, since 60% of Americans are still not connected to the Internet
c   The Japanese CPI excludes common and ever-cheaper mobile phones and personal computers
d   The Russian price index makes inexact allowances for volatile black-market prices

ANSWERS

33 (c) Eliminate the ban on interracial marriage in Alabama

The 200 initiatives and referendums were spread out across 42 states. Most of these were rather mundane measures placed on the ballots by legislatures. A few could have been described as long-overdue tidying-up exercises (Alabamians did indeed decide to eliminate a state constitutional provision banning interracial marriage). But others addressed the kinds of issues that the politicians have been too timid to tackle or too gridlocked to resolve: doctor-assisted suicide (in Maine), background checks for handgun purchases at gun shows (Colorado and Oregon), animal-rights bills, questions of homosexual rights and campaign-finance reforms.

Agents of change, *The Economist*, November 4th 2000

34 (c) The Japanese CPI excludes common and ever-cheaper mobile phones and personal computers

Japan's consumer-price index (CPI) excludes many popular goods such as mobile phones and personal computers, which have fallen sharply in price. An economist at the Bank of Japan estimates that the inflation rate may be overstated by as much as two percentage points. So Japanese consumer prices may be falling by even more than the 0.8% decline reported by the official figures of 2000. What does all this mean for monetary policy? If the gap between different measures of inflation never changed, it would not matter much. But the gap does vary over time. So it is crucial that central banks strive to find and use the most correct measure (and not the most convenient one).

Fighting America's inflation flab, *The Economist*, October 7th 2000

35 "Ranking and spanking" has become popular in the United States. It describes

a   How CEOs, feeling guilty about job losses and their own bonuses, find solace in masochism
b   How troubled firms grade their employees and sack the lowest-rated performers
c   A dangerous form of racing, popular in western states, involving SUVs and large hats
d   How potential MBA students rely on independent ratings when applying to programmes, leaving lower-ranked schools with a smaller talent pool

36 By whom and why was the World Wide Web created?

a   By European physicists, for the sharing of nuclear data
b   By North American universities, for the sharing of library information
c   By the US Department of Defence, for the sharing of military information
d   By teenage computer hackers, for the sharing of stolen information

ANSWERS

35 (b) How troubled firms grade their employees and sack the lowest-rated performers

Downturns have always brought layoffs, but this time the downsizing is different. Rather than cut across the board, companies such as Sun Microsystems, Nortel and Intel ask managers to rank their employees on a bell curve, with the bottom 10–33% found wanting (a process known as "ranking and spanking" or the "hell curve"). In many cases, the bottom decile is at risk of termination for performing badly, which often means no severance. This method is seen by some as a disciplined way to force the issue of performance to the fore. But it can be demoralising and dangerous when applied too quickly, without objective performance criteria to back up subjective rankings.

Dotgone, *The Economist*, March 31st 2001

36 (a) By European physicists, for the sharing of nuclear data

Tim Berners-Lee at CERN, a giant high-energy-physics laboratory straddling the Franco-Swiss border, designed the World Wide Web as a means to disseminate high-energy-physics data. Although some CERN scientists initially balked at the use of this tool for base commercial purposes, the laboratory now happily basks in the glow of the web's success. The only catch is that, although invented in Europe, the web was exploited far more quickly in America. Officials at CERN are easily irked by mention of this, and point out that had the organisation tried to cash in on the technology by making it proprietary, it might not have been adopted so widely.

Cause for conCERN?, *The Economist*, October 28th 2000

QUESTIONS

37 What possible historical fraud had Britons feeling duped?

a Shakespeare's "St Crispin's Day" speech in "Henry V" may derive from a recently discovered French work on Charles I d'Albret, Henry's opponent at Agincourt
b An actor known for his radio work as a talking dachshund may have recorded Churchill's famous speeches to Britain during the Blitz
c A new biography reveals that Nelson may have lost his arm due to his own clumsiness in a cannon exercise near Gibraltar, and not in battle at Tenerife
d The Earl of Sandwich may have stolen the one idea for which he is remembered from Chaucer, who always ate at his desk

38 When the Japanese occupied Hong Kong during the second world war, almost all the territory's trees were chopped down for wood. But environmentalists today can take heart because:

a Hong Kong's temperature has warmed by three-fourths of a degree over the past decade, thus achieving what leading dendrologists say is the optimal temperature to regrow tropical rainforests
b Hong Kong still supports more types of bird, mammal, insect and plant than the whole British Isles
c After the handover, China forced the island's main perfume factory to stop dumping waste in the Pearl River
d Hong Kong's environmental-protection agency is now ranked by Greenpeace second in the world, after Barbados

ANSWERS

37 (b) **An actor known for his radio work as a talking dachshund may have recorded Churchill's famous speeches to Britain during the Blitz**

In 1972 an obscure radio actor, Norman Shelley, claimed to be the voice behind Churchill's "fight on the beaches" speech, a claim bolstered in 1999 when his son stumbled across a 78 rpm record marked "BBC; Churchill speech. Artist: Norman Shelley". Were the British really so cruelly deceived in their finest hour? While Churchill gave the 1940 (unrecorded) speech at the House of Commons, Mr Shelley's might be the version preserved on historical recordings taken from an overseas broadcast in 1942. By then Churchill presumably could not spare the time to re-record his old speeches. Still, it seems that no deception was practised in 1940, which should be enough to let patriotic Brits rest easy in their beds.

His master's voice?, *The Economist*, November 4th 2000

38 (b) **Hong Kong still supports more types of bird, mammal, insect and plant than the whole British Isles**

Hong Kong's 1,095 square kilometres (423 square miles) support more types of bird, mammal, insect and plant than the whole of the British Isles. But only just. The native forests, which had suffered sporadic felling for centuries, were almost annihilated during the Japanese occupation. Though much of the land was replanted (and two-fifths of the territory is now protected as "country parks"), that replanting was usually done with only one or two species, creating so-called monocultures. Moreover, these monocultures were frequently composed of aliens, such as Australian eucalypts, and the one widely employed native species – the Masson pine – has been all but wiped out by pine nematodes, tiny worms that are wreaking havoc in plantations throughout southern China.

Primal dream, *The Economist*, January 9th 1999

QUESTIONS

39 Nokia, the Finnish mobile-phone maker, is one of Europe's brightest business success stories of the past decade. But the company would be unrecognisable to its founders, who established it in 1865 as a:

a Manufacturer of sewer-flow meters
b Fashionable retailer of calico cloth
c Craft shop selling Finnish art, particularly by the artist Minna Nokia, who specialised in the naked body
d Lumber mill on the banks of the Nokia river

40 According to a gripping doctoral thesis on French chocolate-making, who typically runs chocolate-manufacturing houses in south-west France?

a Married couples: the husband makes the chocolate, the wife runs the shop
b Married couples: the wife makes the chocolate, the husband eats it
c Single women weighing more than 90kg
d A German conglomerate, Eurochock, which first made its name marketing maraschino cherries

ANSWERS

39 (d) Lumber mill on the banks of the Nokia river

The process of Nokia's transformation from staid old conglomerate into one of the world's most relentlessly focused consumer-technology companies was relatively slow. A couple of decades ago, the one-time lumber mill was a stodgy Finnish conglomerate, making everything from rubber boots and cables to lavatory paper and televisions. But as early as the late 1970s, the company was already ploughing profits from its traditional operations into buying technology and electronics businesses – mainly computers and TVs. Mobile telephony did not exist as such, but Nokia was already big in radio telephones – an essential communications tool in sparsely populated Scandinavia. When Ericsson adapted an American technology to build an early cellular network in 1980, Nokia was a natural choice to provide the telephones.

A Finnish fable, *The Economist*, October 14th 2000

40 (a) Married couples: the husband makes the chocolate, the wife runs the shop

Susan Terrio, now associate professor of French and anthropology at Georgetown University in Washington, was visiting a Paris *chocolatier* when she recognised that such artisans would make an ideal topic for her doctoral thesis. Probing beneath the smooth dark coating of the luxury craft, she found darker truths concealed. The hierarchical structure of the chocolate manufacturing houses is rigid and sexist. They are invariably run by married couples, the husband making the chocolates and the wife running the shop. Attempts to vary the pattern are resisted, often at the cost of misery and feuding. As a scholar, Ms Terrio tries not to salivate over the products themselves, though she quotes the comments of connoisseurs, often borrowing wine terminology ("sublime, very long on the palate").

Black and bitter, *The Economist*, October 21st 2000

QUESTIONS

41 Which of the following is equivalent to an exabyte?

a   The annual output of all the McDonald's restaurants in the western hemisphere
b   The information in about 20 billion copies of *The Economist*
c   The amount of magical charge required to power ten broomsticks (according to the "Harry Potter" books)
d   The amount of information in about 50m copies of "Harry Potter and the Chamber of Secrets"

42 A failed coup attempt in Ukraine in September 2000 was amateurish in its execution. For example, the maps used by the plotters were apparently guides for:

a   Mushroom hunters
b   Kyiv's nightclubbers
c   Oil-field technicians in neighbouring Kazakhstan
d   New recruits to the women's-studies department at Kyiv Polytechnical Institute

ANSWERS

41 (b) The information in about 20 billion copies of *The Economist*

Already drowning in too much information? At least you can now find out precisely how much you are missing: about two exabytes. (An exabyte is roughly a billion times a billion bytes, or the equivalent of about 20 billion copies of *The Economist*.) This is the estimated amount of unique information the world is currently producing each year, as calculated by a group of researchers at the University of California, Berkeley. But while humanity is producing ever more information, it doesn't consume much more than it did in 1992 – in the United States, at least. The total time American households spend reading, watching television or listening to music increased only slightly from 3,324 hours in 1992 to 3,380 hours in 2000.

Byte counters, *The Economist*, October 21st 2000

42 (a) Mushroom hunters

According to the Ukraine's security service, the USB, the group conceived of a planned attack on the Chernobyl nuclear power station and other key installations, followed by a seizure of power and the restoration of Communist rule. Even viewed within the annals of bungled coup attempts, the effort seemed implausibly crude. Cartographic choices aside, the alleged plotters were a small bunch of retired officers, with no proper plan. Their organisation was well-known, not clandestine. And there is no evidence that they had any weapons. The USB quickly interceded before any mushrooms could be harmed.

Plenty of plots, not much reform, *The Economist*, October 21st 2000

QUESTIONS

43 **Madeleine Albright's visit to Pyongyang in October 2000 was filled with peculiar pleasantries. For example, North Korea's president Kim Jong Il,**

a   Gave her a ring inset with his image carved in micro-mosaic and promised never to target the United States with nuclear weapons
b   Confided that he, like Mr Clinton, would not have turned down Monica Lewinsky
c   Gave her a small silver sea-turtle, North Korea's symbol of peace, but said nothing about nuclear weapons
d   Asked for her e-mail address

44 **Americans' obsession with diet has resulted in a number of myths about food and health. For example,**

a   The makers of All-Bran, a faddish cereal in the 1980s, claimed that it had made hamsters virtually immortal
b   Whoppers reduce the risk of heart attacks, reported the *Wall Street Journal* in 1968
c   In 1974 a doctor in Los Angeles with a popular television show claimed that cancer was caused by orange juice
d   In the 1830s, Sylvester Graham (of Graham cracker fame) claimed that rich and spicy food, together with meat and white bread, excited passions that led to sexual excess

ANSWERS

43 (d) **Asked for her e-mail address**

Rogue pen pals aside, did Mrs Albright achieve anything concrete with her visit? The secretary did not say, volunteering only that when the image of a ballistic-missile launch was superimposed on the wall of the stadium where she was fêted, Mr Kim turned to her and quipped that it was the first such launch and would be the last. Of course, this is a promise that North Korea had already made, and anyway only addresses one of America's numerous concerns about the North's missile programme. But if nothing else, Mrs Albright's visit allowed Mr Kim to meet his first American, and a posse of mostly American journalists to get their first sight of North Korea.

An American in North Korea, *The Economist*, October 28th 2000

44 (d) **In the 1830s, Sylvester Graham (of Graham cracker fame) claimed that rich and spicy food, together with meat and white bread, excited passions that led to sexual excess**

Mr Graham was the pioneer of American food fads. In the 1830s he began preaching the importance of diet in a vigorous life. He encouraged people to bake their own wholewheat bread, convinced that the commercially produced white loaf was too rich to be properly digested. The trend laid the foundation for the breakfast cereals introduced by the Kellogg brothers and their rival Charles Post. Based on suspect nutritional theories and an obsession with regular bowel movements, these and similar new products represented an early triumph of advertising as much as any significant advance in western man's well-being. Throughout most of the 20th century, marketing was the determining factor in the diet of the developed world, with healthy and unhealthy foods being equally touted.

You ate it, Ralph, *The Economist*, November 4th 2000

QUESTIONS

45 According to current convention, the head of the ___ cannot be ___:

a   OECD ... Canadian or Mexican
b   European Central Bank ... German
c   Swedish Carnivore Association ... Swedish
d   UN High Commissioner for Refugees ... Swiss

46 E-mail is an efficient form of communication but tends to gobble up employees' time. Some companies have fought back by:

a   Installing a Microsoft program that copies one in every 18 e-mails to a manager
b   Putting posters in company bathrooms that depict e-mail as the Antichrist
c   Using GroupCries, an e-mail program that administers a low-level electric shock every time a message is sent to more than five addresses
d   Blocking outgoing e-mails for several hours in the morning and afternoon

ANSWERS

45 (b) European Central Bank ... German

The taboo exists because the ECB, based in Frankfurt, was not meant to signal monetary domination of Europe by the Bundesbank. That view looked fine in the old days when the worry was that the euro would be too strong, and that the euro countries might suffer from deflation. No longer. What the euro needs now is credibility. And who has all Europe's monetary credibility? The Bundesbank.

Wim's whim, *The Economist*, October 21st 2000

46 (d) Blocking outgoing e-mails for several hours in the morning and afternoon

Like pornography, e-mail can make the Internet the scourge of corporate efficiency. Michael Schrage, an academic at MIT's Media Lab and author on business innovation, wonders whether companies should give employees an e-mail budget, or at least discover which 20% of the staff send 80% of the e-mails. And in some American companies, sending e-mail with a smutty joke can get you fired. More dangerous than dirt, though, is anger. In a speech in 1999, Michael Eisner, chairman of Walt Disney, argued that e-mail had served to increase the intensity of emotion within his company and become the principal cause of workplace warfare. "With e-mail," he noted, "our impulse is not to file and save, but to click and send."

Handle with care, *The Economist*, November 11th 2000

47 Kennewick man is a subject of controversy because:

a   On average, he drinks and smokes twice as much as the average British male, yet lives five years longer
b   To some anthropologists, his existence suggests that Canada's first inhabitants were interesting
c   Native Americans and scientists are battling over his bones
d   Some of his genetic material appears to come from chickens

48 The *Movimiento Pachacuti*, a new political party, aims to put Bolivia's rural problems into the political spotlight. From where does it take its inspiration?

a   "The Magnificent Seven", a 1960 film starring Yul Brynner and Steve McQueen
b   The life of Chico Pantango, an Indian peasant who was kidnapped and murdered by government paramilitaries in 1999
c   "The soaring condor, the erupting soil of the Altiplano and the divine fecundity of the cocoa bean"
d   The deeds of Tupac Katari, an Indian leader who led a revolt against the Spanish in 1781–83 and was dismembered for his efforts

ANSWERS

47 (c) **Native Americans and scientists are battling over his bones**

At 9,300 years, Kennewick Man is no chicken. But in some ways he is as modern as Madonna. He has, for example, got his own personal website. He is fashionably championed by an array of native American tribes. And he will soon be a key, albeit silent, figure in a pivotal lawsuit. A consortium of tribes claim Kennewick Man as an ancestor under a law that allows them to remove artifacts and ancestors' bones from museum collections. But eight scientists joined legal battle to disagree, arguing there really is no affinity between Kennewick Man, whose origins are thought to be Polynesian, and the modern American tribes of Siberian descent.

Boneheaded, *The Economist*, September 30th 2000

48 (d) **The deeds of Tupac Katari, an Indian leader who led a revolt against the Spanish in 1781–83 and was dismembered for his efforts**

Rural communities on the plains of the Altiplano, which stretch into Chile and Peru as well as Bolivia, live much as their ancestors did, and speak the same Indian language. For them, the casualties of age-old collisions with Bolivia's powerful, among them Mr Katari, remain a potent symbol for the indigenous cause. "We must bring the smell of the coca leaf and the Indian people to parliament," says the party's self-appointed leader, Felipe Quispe, who officially launched the party on the site where Tupac Katari died. And last year's co-ordinated blockade of roads by thousands of rural farmers across the Altiplano loosely copied Mr Katari's strategy against the Spanish. Thankfully for Mr Quispe, however, the resolution was more amicable: he and the government reached a truce to end the conflict.

Inca nation, *The Economist*, October 28th 2000

QUESTIONS

49 India's ambitious drug firms want to crack the worldwide generics market. They may succeed because:

a The Indian government will subsidise the firms' assault with a $3 billion cash injection
b Indian generic drugs are generally held to look more attractive than their western counterparts
c On average, drugs companies in developed countries take 40 times as long to manufacture, market and distribute a new generic
d Indian firms are already accustomed to cut-throat competition (there are some 40 Indian brands of Ranitidine, an anti-ulcer drug)

50 America may have "won" the Sydney Olympics, but adjust the count of the number of medals won for population, or GDP, and the results differ:

a Adjusting by GDP, Cuba won more gold medals than any other country
b Romania produced one gymnastics medal for every 5m citizens (America produced one for every 54m citizens)
c Tweaking the figures for population, Guinea was the overall winner
d Using both GDP and population to adjust the results, Paraguay came top and Japan last

ANSWERS

49 (d) Indian firms are already accustomed to cut-throat competition (there are some 40 Indian brands of Ranitidine, an anti-ulcer drug)

Indian firms are accustomed to the fierce competition that awaits them in rich-country markets. Manufacturing costs are perhaps two-thirds of rich-country levels, a big advantage in such a low-margin business as generic drugs. That has not made India the world's preferred supplier. "Made in India" has been no more a byword for quality in drugs than it has been in cars or consumer electronics. And American drug companies import raw materials from Indian manufacturers, but few finished products such as pills. Indian companies have tried to overcome this hurdle by giving their generics a novel twist, which could be as simple as masking the taste of a bitter pill or as complex as finding new ways of delivering familiar drugs.

Generic genius, *The Economist*, September 30th 2000

50 (a) Adjusting by GDP, Cuba won more gold medals than any other country

With 50 medals for every $100 billion of GDP, Cuba's performance roundly trumped that of the United States, which averaged 1.4 medals per $100 billion. And the results may irritate the Americans in another way, too. Added together, the 15 countries that make up the former Soviet Union garnered 48 gold medals, compared with 39 for the United States. Proportionately, the Bahamas, whose 295,000 citizens carried home one gold medal (shared by their four female relay-runners), won 24 times as many golds as the Americans, who managed only one for every 7m of theirs. Slovenia and Cuba take silver and bronze, respectively, in the medals-per-person tally.

Sydney's secret winners, *The Economist*, October 7th 2000

QUESTIONS

51 **The end may not be so nigh. Which fear about exotic experiments at the Relativistic Heavy Ion Collider in New York state was allayed in November 2000?**

a   The experiments could lead to super-weapons capable of vaporising everything above ground over an area the size of France
b   They could ignite the earth's atmosphere
c   They could turn the earth into an uncomfortably hot "dwarf-bagel" star
d   They could transform the planet into a soup of so-called "strange matter"

52 **Many religions in Russia find themselves frustrated by official obstruction. For example:**

a   The Salvation Army, an organisation of Christian do-gooders, has had to pay over $10,000 fighting a legal battle to register itself
b   Hindus who failed to identify themselves as such upon entering Russia after 1994 were temporarily "resettled" in Tajikistan
c   President Putin has hinted that Russia's Anabaptists may be reclassified as Methodists
d   President Putin has hinted that Russia's Scientologists may be reclassified as Mormons

ANSWERS

51 (d) They could transform the planet into a soup of so-called "strange matter"

Designed to mimic conditions just after the Big Bang, the RHIC experiment accelerates the nuclei of heavy atoms to somewhere close to the speed of light, before smashing them together. The process produces a rare variety of quark known as the "strange" quark. In theory, strange quarks can unite with everyday quarks to form a strangelet, whose very existence, scientists feared, might jump-start a runaway reaction that would transform the entire planet into strange matter. But Jes Madsen, a physicist at the University of Aarhus, has noted that, even if small strangelets were formed, their positive charge would repel normal atomic nuclei, thus precluding the snowball effect that scientists had feared. Time, therefore, to start worrying about something else.

The New York Strangeler, *The Economist*, December 2nd 2000

52 (a) The Salvation Army, an organisation of Christian do-gooders, has had to pay over $10,000 fighting a legal battle to register itself

The Salvation Army is far from the only victim of government hostility towards religion. In official Russian rhetoric, the words "Islamic" and "terrorist" are interchangeable. And although Mr Putin had a well-publicised lunch with the doyen of Soviet-era Jewish *refusniks*, Natan Sharansky, anti-Semitism in Russia provokes rather mild official objections. When the governor of the Kursk region, Alexander Mikhailov, said the president supported his fight against Jewish "filth", the Kremlin rebuked him, but merely for "foolishness". By Soviet standards, Russia is incomparably freer than it used to be. But by the standards of western democracies, there is some cause for concern; and those concerns are growing, rather than diminishing.

How free is free?, *The Economist*, November 25th 2000

QUESTIONS

53 **The 1876 US presidential contest between Samuel Tilden, a Democrat, and Rutherford Hayes, a Republican, was exceptionally dirty. For example, it was alleged that Hayes:**

a   Murdered his mother in a fit of insanity
b   Deliberately spread syphilis to five lovers and a cat
c   Dodged the draft for the north in the Civil War
d   Would have flunked Harvard Law School had his father not been the Dean

54 **Family businesses are the commonest type of corporate structure. According to Sir Adrian Cadbury, author of a guide to the proper way to run such firms, their crises usually come when:**

a   The company appoints an outsider to a senior job (especially if it is a woman)
b   The firm's patriarch hands over to the second generation
c   The second generation hands over to the third
d   One family member kills another

ANSWERS

53 (a) Murdered his mother in a fit of insanity

Hayes's supporters responded in kind to the impressive double calumny. They charged that Tilden, the Democratic governor from New York, was at heart a syphilitic swindler. Tilden won 51% of the popular vote and came just one short of a majority in the electoral college. But the votes in three southern states were disputed (Florida was one), and all three eventually sent competing returns to Congress. The House and Senate, however, were controlled by different parties and could not agree on which votes to certify. So they set up a bipartisan commission to settle their disputes. Hayes was elected amid universal accusations of fraud and sporadic violence. (Somebody shot at Hayes while he was at dinner.) He served one term.

Watch yourself at dinner, Dubya, *The Economist*, November 25th 2000

54 (b) The firm's patriarch hands over to the second generation

Given the trauma of passing on a business, it is not surprising that those who write about family firms choose titles such as "Succeeding Generations" for their works. They might as well have picked "King Lear". When Sir Adrian toured the world to talk about his views on corporate governance, he constantly bumped into families wondering what to do with their business. "Crunch time", he says, "is when the patriarch hands over to the second generation. At that point, the failure rate is highest." Kelin Gersick, another expert in the field, thinks the transition from second generation to third can be almost as perilous. Ownership often passes from the founder's heirs – siblings who have grown up with the same family culture – to a looser network of cousins.

Lear's curse, *The Economist*, December 2nd 2000

QUESTIONS

55 **Scientists at the University of Virginia exposed fruit flies to purified "freebase" cocaine in late 1999. What happened?**

a   Some fruit flies were more susceptible to addiction than others
b   Several scientists were loth to waste cocaine on the flies and attempted to snort the drugged insects
c   Over time, larger drug doses were necessary for a fly high
d   The fruit flies most vulnerable to the drug reacted positively to music with strong rhythms

56 **Which novel did Tony Blair pick for his hypothetical stay on a deserted island for the BBC Radio programme, "Desert Island Discs"?**

a   "Portnoy's Complaint", by Philip Roth
b   "Ivanhoe", by Sir Walter Scott
c   "Bridget Jones's Diary", by Helen Fielding
d   "Sybil, or The Two Nations", by Benjamin Disraeli

ANSWERS

55 **(a) Some fruit flies were more susceptible to addiction than others**
Cocaine has a "reverse tolerance" effect: rather than becoming accustomed to cocaine with increasing exposure (as happens with, say, alcohol), the brain becomes more sensitive and therefore more hooked. In humans, studying cocaine sensitisation is tricky since most governments have strong views on giving drugs to the uninitiated. So instead researchers turned to creatures such as the fruit fly, *Drosophila melanogaster*, to probe the cellular basis for cocaine craving. The team found that mutant *Drosophila* lacking certain genes known to control circadian rhythm did not experience "reverse tolerance". If the propensity to addiction is also genetically controlled in humans, it could provide a mechanism to address the problem at the cellular level.

Flying high, *The Economist*, August 14th 1999

56 **(b) "Ivanhoe", by Sir Walter Scott**
The selection got him labelled a philistine. Sir John Drummond specifically (and viciously) attacked the prime minister's affinity for the corny novel in the course of a larger slandering of Labour's treatment of the high arts. This sort of criticism is both snooty and inaccurate, since there is scant evidence that ministers' own tastes have had much influence on how money for the arts has been distributed. Some added attention and cash have been devoted to the film industry, but the proportion of Arts Council funds dedicated to the various art forms has remained relatively constant. And despite Mr Blair's blokeish enthusiasm for football, his government still spends more than four times as much on the arts as it does on sport.

Philistines in high places, *The Economist*, August 19th 2000

QUESTIONS

57 Why should deep-sea divers remember to keep their teeth in good condition?

a Changes in pressure can cause weak teeth to explode
b To pay tribute to the late Jacques Cousteau, who often lectured his crew on dental hygiene
c The gleam of white teeth is more likely to scare away underwater threats, such as sharks
d Exposed calcium from cavities can make decompression sickness worse

58 A Roper Starch Worldwide poll in September 2000 asked respondents how much time they spent thinking about their appearance, and compiled a "vanity index". Of the following nations, which proved the most vain?

a Japan (mainly on account of its men)
b The United States
c South Africa
d France (mainly on account of its women)

ANSWERS

57 (a) Changes in pressure can cause weak teeth to explode

The same goes for hang-gliders. Even for divers with pearly whites, extreme changes in pressure can lead to decompression sickness ("the bends"). But mankind has frequently proven adept at adopting animals' tricks to survive otherwise fatal conditions. Taking ten minutes at the surface between dives, for example, can prevent the bends; sperm whales use a similar tactic. And in a pinch, strong teeth can also come in handy. An 1862 adventurer in a hot-air balloon, when paralysed by altitude sickness, used his teeth to pull the rope to vent hydrogen from the balloon.

On the edge, *The Economist*, July 15th 2000

58 (c) South Africa

With just under 40% of its population thinking "all the time" about their looks, South Africa ranked fifth in national vanity. Only Turkey, Russia, Mexico and leader Venezuela come closer to narcissus. To those in the know, Venezuela's 60% showing is hardly a surprise. After all, the nation also holds the record for deodorant-use and its citizens spend an average of 20% of household income on personal-care products. Observers of New York fashion extravaganzas may be surprised to find that Americans, while easily beating the Japanese and French, do not reach vanity's top tier; a meagre 22% claim to be perpetually preoccupied with their looks.

Vanity, *The Economist*, September 2nd 2000

QUESTIONS

59 Richard Nixon was accused of many things. Which of the following allegations was actually true?

a As a senator, he blackmailed his adulterous chief of staff
b He usually gave cheaper wine to his senior advisers than he served himself
c He made several racist comments about John F. Kennedy's dog
d He did not like soap

60 "Euthanasia" is a gentle death. What was "Ruthanasia"?

a A spate of economic reforms in New Zealand, championed by then-finance minister Ruth Richardson, in 1990–91
b A series of advertisements used by New York's mayor, Rudolph Giuliani, to defeat his Democratic opponent, Ruth Messinger, in 1997
c The title of a novel by Cynthia Ozick, starring the character Ruth Puttermesser
d The nickname Columbia Law School students gave to the grading system of future Supreme Court justice Ruth Bader Ginsburg

ANSWERS

59 **(b) He usually gave cheaper wine to his senior advisers than he served himself**

On October 7th 1972, Henry Kissinger and Le Duc Tho agreed on the essential terms to end the Vietnam war. President Nixon was so ebullient that he departed from his usual practice and actually shared his Lafite Rothschild. (Almost all other occasions saw the president save the good stuff for himself.) But the South Vietnamese government, ill-informed of the course of the negotiations, feared that the settlement would endanger its survival and refused to acquiesce. As talks dragged, secretary of state Henry Kissinger ordered large-scale bombing of the North, alienating Tho. They met again on January 8th 1973, at which Tho declared, "You ... stained the honour of the United States." One suspects Mr Nixon then served Mr Kissinger a bitter wine indeed.

Unsparing, *The Economist*, December 2nd 2000

60 **(a) A spate of economic reforms in New Zealand, championed by then-finance minister Ruth Richardson, in 1990–91**

In the mid-1980s, New Zealand's economy was on an unsustainable course, with enormous budget and current-account deficits and mounting inflationary pressures that were masked by price controls. It was also the most distorted economy in the OECD. Almost all its prices, which in market economies are supposed to send signals to firms and individuals, were controlled, and high trade barriers shielded inefficient producers from competition. Enter Roger Douglas, finance minister of the Labour government after 1984. "Rogernomics" consisted of both microeconomic reform and macroeconomic stabilisation. But by 1987, "Rogernomics" had run its course, with still more work to be done. Thus the stage was set for "Ruthanasia" which took place under the National government's finance minister, Ruth Richardson, in 1990–91.

Can the Kiwi economy fly?, *The Economist*, December 2nd 2000

61 In many ways, Jeffrey Immelt, General Electric's boss-in-waiting, resembles GE's current chief, Jack Welch. Like Mr Welch, he:

a   At first refused to take stock options upon joining GE
b   Always orders a Philly cheesesteak at the GE cafeteria, according to his official biography, "Immelt by Nature"
c   Spent his formative corporate years being moulded in GE's plastics division
d   Has fired about one-sixth of the employees directly under his supervision, yet still manages to be popular

62 Some old stereotypes about Germans no longer hold true. For example:

a   Germany produced more comedy films than any other country in Europe, beating Britain by 11% in 2000
b   Urban traffic accidents are up 23% over the past decade, as Germans become more willing to break the rules
c   German food is the second-best in Europe: Germany now has five chefs with Michelin's coveted three-star rating, more than any European country bar France
d   In a recent international competition, German beers were trumped by American ones in the final medal count

ANSWERS

61 (c) Spent his formative corporate years being moulded in GE's plastics division

At first glance, Mr Immelt appears to be a Welch clone. Like Mr Welch, he is taking over at the age of 45, which allows a 20-year run before retirement. Also like Mr Welch, he spent his formative corporate years in GE's plastics division. And the two men share a passion for such management dogma as work-outs and the shift from products to services. But dig deeper and some slight differences start to appear. Mr Immelt may be cut from Welchian cloth, but it is of a softer variety. Where Mr Welch is a confrontational terrier, Mr Immelt is a bear of a man known for his teasing good humour. Look for "softer" changes – for more non-Americans, more women and fewer suits at the top of GE.

The man who would be Jack, *The Economist*, December 2nd 2000

62 (c) German food is the second-best in Europe: Germany now has five chefs with Michelin's coveted three-star rating, more than any European country bar France

Most people outside Germany think of German food as, at best, a joke. Ah, yes. There is *Sauerkraut* (pickled cabbage), *Eisbein* (a fatty knuckle of pork), *Kartoffelsuppe* (potato soup), and more than 300 types of sausage – outscoring, if only in quantity, General de Gaulle's 246 varieties of French cheese. But *haute cuisine*? Surely not. So gourmands with delicate palates and sniffy noses may be shocked to discover that Germany now has more chefs honoured with the Michelin Guide's top three-star rating than any other country in Europe, bar France. And no, these wonder-chefs are not all imported: three of the five that have been acclaimed are native Germans.

So Germans can be gourmets too, *The Economist*, December 9th 2000

QUESTIONS

63 Has recycling gone too far? Research is now underway that would allow recyclers to turn:

a Dead fish into disposable nappies (diapers)
b Sewage into pillow stuffing
c Compost into cake filling
d Liposuctioned human fat into soap

64 Britain needs more runway space, but many residents near airports are resisting – understandably. Which of the following has fallen out of aircraft near Heathrow in recent years?

a Four frozen human bodies and two tons of fish stock
b Two human bodies and quantities of frozen human excrement
c A tennis racket, three sneakers and a stuffed partridge
d Innumerable slivers of metal from airplanes' rear hatches, which typically cleave off during heavy rains

ANSWERS

63 (a) Dead fish into disposable nappies (diapers)

Babies, beware: Srinivasan Damodaran, a food scientist, knows how to make an eco-friendly filler for disposable nappies (diapers in America) out of "bycatch", the nearly 20m tonnes of fish caught each year that is unsuitable for sale. Dr Damodaran extracts protein from the fish and then treats it with a chemical known as EDTAD that lends it superb absorbency. Not only does this make use of dead fish that would otherwise be dumped into the sea to decompose and pollute coastal areas, but, unlike their synthetic counterparts, fish-based nappies are easily broken down by the fungi and bacteria that populate landfills. Only a few squeamish parents stand in the way of an environmental triumph.

Smells fishy, *The Economist* Technology Quarterly, December 9th 2000

64 (b) Two human bodies and quantities of frozen human excrement

The British government is in a bind. More people want to fly, but nobody wants an airport anywhere near home. Public concern over noise, traffic, safety and pollution is growing – hardly surprising considering what's fallen from aircraft coming in to land at Heathrow in the past five years. But the pressure to expand London airports is growing rapidly. The growth of budget operators such as EasyJet, Go, Ryanair and Virgin Express has caused budget passenger numbers to grow 50% a year over the past three years. And the London Chamber of Commerce predicts that current runway capacity at all London airports will be exhausted within the next ten years.

The problems stack up, *The Economist*, December 9th 2000

QUESTIONS

65 So pleased were American women to gain the vote in 1920 that they commissioned a statue of three suffragette leaders. It was supposed to stand in the entrance to the Capitol. Where is it?

a Congressmen dubbed it "Three Ladies in a Bathtub" and stashed it away in a crypt
b In Lourdes, south-west France, where three miracles have been attributed to it
c The statue shattered after being knocked over in the great hurricane of 1947
d After standing for nearly ten years, a congressional order deemed it "unattractive" and it was demolished

66 In 2000 *The Economist* conducted a self-reporting survey of cabinet ministers in Britain and Germany to discover their linguistic abilities. The survey found that:

a The entire German cabinet was at least bilingual. Most of the British cabinet were too embarrassed to respond to the survey
b John Prescott, Britain's deputy prime minister, and Nick Brown, then its agriculture minister, could speak only English (though Mr Prescott employs his own, idiosyncratic dialect)
c No member of the German cabinet could speak both Nepalese and Estonian. Two British ministers could
d Apart from English, British ministers were more likely to speak dead languages than living ones

ANSWERS

65 **(a) Congressmen dubbed it "Three Ladies in a Bathtub" and stashed it away in a crypt**

America in the early decades of the 20th century was awash with talk of social change: for blacks and other downtrodden groups as well as giving women the same freedom as men. In 1918 British women were given the vote, and the United States followed in 1920. But the men seem to have yielded more from exhaustion than enthusiasm. America's triumphant women commissioned a statue of three suffragette leaders to stand in the entrance of the Capitol building, the home of Congress. But congressmen mockingly dubbed the statue "Three Ladies in a Bathtub" and put it in the crypt. In 1999 the statue was given a dusting and put on display, although its future is still unclear.

Ruth Dyk, *The Economist*, December 9th 2000

66 **(b) John Prescott, then Britain's deputy prime minister, and Nick Brown, then its agriculture minister, could speak only English (though Mr Prescott employed his own, idiosyncratic dialect)**

At least Tony Blair speaks French, and has earned great approbation by doing so in France – confirming the view that French surliness towards the British evaporates if the latter make a little effort. The prime minister has also picked up some Italian on his holidays. The Germans, by contrast, are more cosmopolitan. Several of them speak more than one foreign language. One knows some Hebrew. They are also happier to publicise their language skills. All of them responded to *The Economist*'s inquiries, whereas a surprising number of British ministers rebuffed them. Even Peter Mandelson, then probably the cabinet's most ardent Europhile, chose not to reveal his talents (if he had them).

Parlez-vous Anglais?, *The Economist*, December 16th 2000

QUESTIONS

67 Geoff Hiscock first published "Asia's New Wealth Club" in 1997, just before Asia's financial storm. How many billionaires on his list failed to make the second edition of the book, published in 2000?

a   Just five, all of them in the property business
b   28 out of 100 on the original list
c   39 out of 50 on the original list
d   All 100 on the original list

68 In 1995, Banco Comercial Portugues decided to expand its Lisbon headquarters. Which of the following was not found in its basement during renovation?

a   Evidence of a Phoenician settlement
b   A Christian grave dating from the 5th century
c   A Roman temple for vestal virgins
d   A Roman fish-processing factory

ANSWERS

67 (b) 28 out of 100 on the original list

With remarkably unlucky timing, Geoff Hiscock published the first edition of his guide to Asia's billionaires in 1997, just as the financial storm that started in Thailand and soon swept through the whole region was gathering speed. Of Mr Hiscock's original top 100 dollar-billionaires, 28 have not survived into his second edition, and all the rankings have changed. Mr Hiscock's richest Asian, for example, is no longer the Sultan of Brunei but Masayoshi Son, hardly a household name. A Japanese businessman, he made $18 billion from Internet companies and has so far successfully ridden out the turbulence in the dotcom markets. (Will the oil-rich sultan have overtaken Mr Son since this book went to press? Further editions beckon.)

Naming names, *The Economist*, October 14th 2000

68 (c) A Roman temple for vestal virgins

As the bulldozers moved in to make room for garages in the basement, they unearthed some unexpected treasures. Besides some 18th-century sewers, a fifth-century Christian grave and evidence of a Phoenician settlement, the bankers found a Roman fish-processing factory and part of the mosaic floor of the owner's house. These discoveries now form part of a museum in the bank's offices that is open to the public. Oddly enough, BCP is as young as its discoveries are ancient. It was set up a mere 15 years ago, at the time when Portugal was issuing its first private banking licences since the revolution. From scratch, it has already become Portugal's biggest financial institution.

Big fish in small ponds, *The Economist*, December 2nd 2000

QUESTIONS

69 The king of London statues is King Edward VII: there are nine of him scattered around the city. Who is runner-up?

a   Charles Dickens (seven), who just beat Charles I (six)
b   Queen Victoria (seven), with Churchill in third place (four)
c   Sherlock Holmes (four), who just beat Bertrand Russell (three)
d   The Duke of Wellington (seven), who almost didn't beat Napoleon (none)

70 Europeans take plenty of days off and Americans work like dogs. Yeah, yeah. According to a survey by UBS, a Swiss bank, which of the following is true of Chile's labour force?

a   Chileans are the hardest-working people in the world
b   Chileans are the best-paid people in the developing world
c   Chileans take the longest "working" lunches (and drink the most red wine during lunch) of anyone except the Spanish
d   Second to the Senegalese, Chileans are "the least likely to think about work away from the office"

ANSWERS

69 (b) **Queen Victoria (seven), with Churchill in third place (four)**
Putting up statues in city squares or avenues is a way of honouring the heroes of the immediate past. In London the taste for public statuary reached its height at the cusp of the Victorian-Edwardian period, when monarchs, statesmen and, above all, soldiers exemplified the spirit of the age. This explains why King Edward VII has so many statues in his honour, and why Queen Victoria is the leading lady of London statuary. Despite being a good deal more recent and a great deal less sculpted, Winston Churchill, whose London images number four, stands above a field that includes Darwin, Charles I and Thomas More, who have three statues apiece.

Set in stone, *The Economist*, December 9th 2000

70 (a) **Chileans are the hardest-working people in the world**
New York may be the city that never sleeps, but people in a score of other metropolises around the globe spend a lot more time at work. The world's hardest-working population resides in Santiago, Chile. Measured across a variety of professions, the average worker in Santiago clocked 2,244 hours this year with only 17 days of paid holiday. New Yorkers toiled for an average of 1,882 hours. Work rates were also high across Asia and the up-and-coming economies of Latin America. At the other end of the spectrum, the average Parisian worked for only 1,587 hours and took 28 days off with pay. The vacation capitals of the world, however, are Amsterdam, Frankfurt and Madrid: each offers an average of 31 days' holiday.

Labour hours, *The Economist*, December 23rd 2000

QUESTIONS

71 Some prices have risen dramatically in real terms in the past century; others have fallen sharply. All of the following are true, except one. Which is false?

a The price of a pork chop has risen slightly more than the price of *The Economist*
b The price of a three-minute phone call between New York and Chicago has dropped 99%
c The price of a Steinway grand piano has dropped by 60%
d The price of a bicycle has dropped about 70%

72 Which of the following are all names of cars manufactured by Skoda Auto, the largest car manufacturer in Central Europe?

a Fabia, Felicia and Brunnhilde
b Clara, Helena and Sofia
c Fabia, Felicia and Octavia
d Gennifer, Paula and Monica

ANSWERS

71 (c) The price of a Steinway grand piano has dropped by 60%

Over time, general inflation tends to mask changes in individual prices. Strip out the general rise, and variations are clearer. Goods or services that have benefited from large productivity gains, thanks to technological improvements and mass production, have seen large price falls in real terms. Telephone calls are the most striking example. But electricity, bicycles, cars, even eggs (thanks to battery hens) also have fallen. Over the past century, the price of a Steinway grand piano has increased by 160% in real terms. But the true cost of pleasure to a music-lover has tumbled: he buys a compact-disc player instead of a piano, paying less than 1% of the price of a modern Steinway.

The price of age, *The Economist*, December 23rd 2000

72 (c) Fabia, Felicia and Octavia

The Czech word *skoda* means pity or shame. Thus, on spying a passing Skoda car, Czechs used to say "there goes a shame", and nobody would much argue. Skoda's press officer is one Milan Smutny, whose family name means sad. But although jokes about Mr Sad at Shame Inc worked nicely in former Communist times, these days they fall rather flat. With a redesigned fleet that includes the sleek Fabia, bestselling Felicia, and spacious Octavia, Skoda has become the driving force, so to speak, behind the Czech economy, making a respectable profit of $75m in 2000 despite a three-year recession in the Czech Republic.

Slav Motown, *The Economist*, January 6th 2001

QUESTIONS

73 Research suggests that the "angel's share" can vary from 3% to as much as 8%. The term "angel's share" means:

a   The part of a syndicated loan that is underwritten by the lead bank
b   The liquid lost through evaporation during the maturation of whisky
c   The proportion of infants who die in the first year after birth
d   The proportion of a neutrino's mass that is lost when it encounters a charmed quark on a dark night

74 Entertainment robots are set to become a big industry. Which of the following robots was not on sale to the general Japanese public at Christmas 2000?

a   Aibo: a $1,500 performing lion cub
b   Wuvluv: an unpleasant-looking furry animal that lays eggs
c   Dingdong: a frog that eats real flies
d   Wonderborg: an incredibly slow cockroach

ANSWERS

73 (b) The liquid lost through evaporation during the maturation of whisky

Once a barrel is filled with newly made whisky, it is stuck in a warehouse to mature for years. The liquid lost through evaporation is known as the "angel's share", and is unmistakable to the nose of anyone walking into a whisky warehouse. Far from being a loss to be regretted, however, this heavenly tithe is an indication that all is well. If the angels don't take their share, the rest is not worth drinking, as it suggests a problem with that particular barrel and its contents. After four to six years – and generally not many more if all has gone well – what is left can be bottled and sold to an eager world.

The water of life, *The Economist*, December 23rd 2000

74 (c) Dingdong: a frog that eats real flies

Sony boasts that its groundbreaking Aibo can express six emotions: joy, surprise, anger, sadness, fear and dislike. And thanks to the almost infinite possible combination of emotions and sensory inputs (including audio, visual, temperature, infra-red, touch and vibration), Aibo's behaviour is unpredictable. For those who cannot afford Aibo's $1,500 price tag, toy shops have been filling their shelves with no end of cheap derivatives: assorted dogs, a nervous hamster called Cookie, and the unsettling Wuvluvs and Wonderborgs. Another Christmas fad, destined to gather dust in the cupboard like all those wretched Furby dolls? Perhaps, but corporations such as Sony and Honda have bet millions on the market for entertainment robots.

Dr Doi's useless inventions, *The Economist*, December 23rd 2000

QUESTIONS

75 "It would have been an honourable and virtuous act on the part of England to have declared that this should not be." So said philosopher John Stuart Mill about:

a Austria's refusal to give Hungary more power in 1848–49
b The Peterloo massacre of 1819
c Race riots in New Orleans and Memphis, in which hundreds of newly freed slaves were killed
d The apparent death of Sherlock Holmes in "The Final Problem"

76 In the late 1970s, Alfred Kahn, economic adviser to then-president, Jimmy Carter, was told that he was using the word "recession" too often. In his next speech, for "recession," he substituted the word:

a Jabberwock
b Horseradish
c Nincompoop
d Banana

ANSWERS

75 (a) Austria's refusal to give Hungary more power in 1848–49

When deciding how to handle future Kosovos, it serves well to remember the opinion of John Stuart Mill, a political philosopher much respected by the early *Economist*. In general, Mill thought intervention a foolish business. But in 1848–49, when the Hungarians rebelled against the "foreign yoke" of Austrian rule, and then Austria (with Russian help) hauled them back under the yoke, Mill came to the conclusion that England should act. He might have argued that if it becomes reasonably obvious that a government has decided to hold on to power against the wishes of most of the people it governs, and is not going to change its mind, it should not think that its denial of the democratic principle will be allowed to go unchallenged.

Why and when to go in, *The Economist*, January 6th 2001

76 (d) Banana

George Bush junior and his team have been accused of undermining confidence by using the R-word too often. Mr Bush might take a tip from Alfred Kahn, who discussed the risk of America going into a banana, perhaps even one that recalled the Great Banana of the 1930s. Absurd, to be sure, but Kahn's critics may have been on to something. A decade ago *The Economist* proposed the R-word index: an alternative indicator of economic activity at a time of widespread distrust of official British statistics. Using a computer database, we counted for each quarter how many stories in British newspapers had the word "recession". The index closely mirrored the economic cycle.

Rrrrrrrecession?, *The Economist*, January 6th 2001

77 **What method is used by Dr Erik Viirre, of the University of California, San Diego, to relieve the symptoms of vertigo?**

a   He has invented a small device for the "vestibule" of the inner ear to compensate for confused signals to the brain
b   He slows down the perceived world of his patients using virtual-reality goggles
c   He forces his patients to run up bell towers, thus weakening the so-called "Hitchcock reflex"
d   He administers a slight electric shock whenever a patient's vestibular-ocular reflex goes wonky

78 **Thanks in part to movements in the euro, some European cities are much cheaper than is usually assumed. Which of the following is true (as of December 2000), according to the Economist Intelligence Unit?**

a   Prague is cheaper than Manila
b   Frankfurt is cheaper than Cairo
c   Paris is cheaper than Lagos
d   Warsaw is cheaper than Mumbai

ANSWERS

77 **(b) He slows down the perceived world of his patients using virtual-reality goggles**

Vertigo is the result of damage to the body's balancing mechanism. When nerves in the ear sense that the head is moving one way, they tell the eyes to move the opposite way to compensate. Sufferers of vertigo have a slow vestibular-ocular reflex (VOR). This causes their gaze to slide along with the movement of their heads, leaving them confused and nauseous. By placing patients in a virtual environment, Dr Viirre is able to slow down objects in their field of vision. He then gradually accelerates the scene to coax a patient's VOR out of its lazy habits. Helping to rehabilitate vertigo sufferers will show that virtual reality is good for something other than playing games.

A new kind of pacemaker, *The Economist*, February 9th 2001

78 **(b) Frankfurt is cheaper than Cairo**

Tokyo remains the world's priciest city, with living costs more than 50% higher than New York's. And if not for the soaring prices in troubled Belgrade, Asian cities would capture the top four places in the survey: Tokyo is followed by Belgrade, then Hong Kong, Seoul and Taipei. Perhaps more surprising is the performance of cities in South America. Thanks to the weakness of the euro for most of 2000, it now costs more to live in Buenos Aires than in Paris, and Caracas, like Cairo, is a pricier posting than Frankfurt. So cash-poor Europeans might want to sit tight.

Living costs, *The Economist*, January 20th 2001

QUESTIONS

79 **Who have been described as "a bunch of fat, stupid, ugly old ladies that watch soap operas, play bingo, read tabloids and don't know the metric system"?**

a   The Beardstown Ladies Investment Club, by Warren Buffett
b   New Hampshire voters, by Tom Alciere, a New Hampshire state representative
c   Readers of *Oprah* magazine, by Oprah Winfrey
d   The Kremlin's cleaning staff, by Vladimir Putin

80 **Britain's Home Office has been eager to diminish the role of juries in criminal courts. Not only are they slow, expensive and unreliable, it is claimed, but sometimes plain barmy. For instance:**

a   Mary Hiney, a juror in a 1994 arson trial, burned down her house while trying to recreate the crime
b   Jurors in a 1998 case at Snaresbrook crown court acquitted a woman of drug-dealing after she was caught with 2,000 Ecstasy pills, accepting her explanation that she believed them to be extra-strong mints
c   In 1993 a jury at Hove crown court unanimously convicted a man of two murders, after having used an Ouija board to get in touch with one of the victims
d   A 1994 murder prosecution collapsed after jurors spent a night getting drunk on champagne instead of coming to a verdict

ANSWERS

79 (b) New Hampshire voters, by Tom Alciere, a New Hampshire state representative

Compared with the glamorous thrill of the presidential primary, state elections in New Hampshire do not grip the voter. That, at least, is the current explanation of how Tom Alciere, an online advocate of killing policemen, won a seat in the state legislature. At first, Mr Alciere refused to leave his seat, insisting he was "not a nut". Then he said that he would step down only after his pet bills came to a roll-call vote. He wants to legalise drugs, ban involuntary commitments to mental institutions, and replace state schools with online education. Another Republican agreed to submit eight of his proposals, and Mr Alciere resigned. Some think he should have been kept around – to remind voters that they sometimes get what they deserve.

The voters could have known, *The Economist*, January 13th 2001

80 (c) In 1993 a jury at Hove crown court unanimously convicted a man of two murders, after having used an Ouija board to get in touch with one of the victims

Juries are unreliable creatures. Sometimes they put two fingers up to the law. Last year, for instance, 28 Greenpeace campaigners were tried on charges of criminal damage. They admitted destroying six acres of genetically modified maize. The jury found them not guilty. Sometimes what impels them to reach a decision is downright criminal. In 1993 Stephen Young was unanimously convicted by a jury at Hove crown court of two murders and jailed for life. It later emerged that four of the jurors held a séance with an Ouija board to get in touch with one of the victims. Mr Young was promptly retried. Even without the testimony from the beyond, a second jury found him guilty.

Straw condemns the juries, *The Economist*, January 13th 2001

81 "He lets the days pass without concerning himself with anything other than political squabbles, and all the signs are that he is too addicted to drink and women." Who wrote this in a private diary, and about whom?

a   An American State Department official, about the North Korean leader, Kim Jong Il
b   Bill Clinton, about Jesse Jackson
c   Che Guevara, about one of his Congo trainees, Laurent Kabila
d   The former head of Magdalen College, Oxford, about William Hague in his university days

82 Between them, Greek and Japanese shipping lines own more than 30% of the world's merchant tonnage. Perhaps surprisingly:

a   Iran's merchant fleet is larger than Singapore's
b   Switzerland's merchant fleet is larger than France's
c   Germany has no merchant fleet
d   Switzerland has one merchant ship, which is used solely to transport banknotes

ANSWERS

81 (c) Che Guevara, about one of his Congo trainees, Laurent Kabila

After a lifetime spent making revolution in the Congo, Laurent Kabila declared himself president in 1997. In power Mr Kabila quickly showed that he had learned nothing since the days of his Cuban ties, and had forgotten nothing. His main rival was killed in a mysterious ambush. Another died later and the third he imprisoned. He spoke the language of the one-party state and tried to control policy, the economy and the people's thoughts. He deeply mistrusted western governments and their financial institutions and companies. Clumsily trying to play one off against another, he alienated them all. Kabila died in January 2001. His legacy to Congo is a civil war in which six other African nations are involved.

Laurent Kabila, *The Economist*, January 20th 2001

82 (b) Switzerland's merchant fleet is larger than France's

Those with only casual knowledge of the merchant fleet business are probably unaware of the shipping prominence of the Swiss. Their bulk surpasses not only the French but the Spanish and Australians as well. Iran's merchant tonnage is even higher, despite the difficulty in getting their vessels foreign-flagged. But neither country can approach Greece and Japan, whose shipping lines own more than 30% of the world's merchant tonnage. Though total tonnage has increased, the average age of merchant ships has declined. This is especially true of developing countries' container vessels, whose average age fell from 11.4 years to 9.1 years. For the many European nations saddled with outdated fleets, the choice becomes a question of priorities: to shape up or ship out.

Shipping, *The Economist*, February 10th 2001

QUESTIONS

83 **In Brazil priests sometimes use unorthodox methods to draw in the faithful. Father Marcelo Rossi has attracted as many as 1m people to his Sao Paulo masses by:**

a   Presenting a children's programme beforehand, co-hosted by a Brazilian actress, Xuxa
b   Interspersing his masses with aerobics
c   Performing group marriages of up to 1,000 couples at once
d   Handing out free lottery tickets

84 **Absolut Vodka, now one of the world's most successful spirit brands, has come a long way from the days when its bottle was likened to a hospital plasma bag. Which of the following was an Absolut turning point?**

a   Annie Leibovitz photographed Salman Rushdie clutching a burning ad for Absolut
b   Picasso painted an Absolut bottle being emptied over a bed of snakes
c   Madonna serenaded a bottle of Absolut in a video
d   Marlon Brando shattered a bottle of Absolut over a woman's head in the play "A Streetcar Named Desire"

ANSWERS

83 (b) Interspersing his masses with aerobics

He had to do something. In Brazil, the biggest and most influential Catholic country in Latin America, the proportion of people calling themselves Catholic fell from 93% in 1950 to 83% in 1991, the most recent census; it is perhaps another ten percentage points lower now. And within that 70% or so, large numbers will be Catholic in name only. In every region, mass attendance has been falling for the past two decades as modern life makes it harder to dedicate Sundays to prayer. For traditionalists, the general trends are discouraging. Perhaps no less so are the exceptions, such as the masses laced with aerobics that attract as many as 1m people to Rossi's rock-star ministry.

Between this world and the next, The Economist, January 27th 2001

84 (a) Annie Leibovitz photographed Salman Rushdie clutching a burning ad for Absolut

How did a state-run liquor monopoly in Sweden – a country which restricts booze ads to matchboxes – come to own one of the hippest, most successful spirits brands in the world? And how did the Swedes pull this off with Russia's national drink? The story of Absolut vodka is a perfect illustration of modern advertising – the creation of something out of nothing. Absolut's image broke the rules. Its ostentatiously simple, go-anywhere ads (a bottle with a bow-tie, for example, over the slogan "Absolut Elegance") were at odds with the burnished, regional imagery that sold most booze. Then came the high-end names. Andy Warhol painted the bottle. Among many celebrity endorsers, Annie Leibovitz's photographs featuring Salman Rushdie helped make the company into a world hit.

What bottle, The Economist, February 17th 2001

QUESTIONS

85 **Pakistan (joining Iran and the Sudan) was set to impose Islamic banking on its citizens from July 2001. Because the Koran forbids the collection of interest, Pakistani banks are likely to:**

a   Go bust
b   Receive goods or services, rather than cash interest, in payment for loans
c   Require those defaulting on loans to provide compensation in the form of a period of enforced servitude
d   Buy capital goods, such as machinery, for a customer and then sell them to the customer for a higher price and keep the difference

86 **Amazon.com's egalitarian approach to book reviews – anybody can write one – has provided plenty of opportunity for mischief. For example:**

a   Reviewers of "Nymphomania: a hystory" used the site to post their e-mail addresses, telephone numbers and preferences
b   Eric Goldman, a university professor, wrote 43 anonymous reviews praising his own turgid "The Mysterious Raccoon". By the time Amazon found out, the site had sold 2,000 copies
c   Some 18,000 reviewers blasted Michael Bellesiles's book, "Arming America", after the NRA gun lobby asked members to post their thoughts
d   Somebody submitted a review of the Bible and signed it "God". Once Amazon had removed this, another review was posted which opined that the Bible "is not as good as the film"

ANSWERS

85 **(d) Buy capital goods, such as machinery, for a customer and then sell them to the customer for a higher price and keep the difference**

The Koran clearly condemns interest, which is called *riba* in Arabic, as exploitative and unjust. So instead of paying interest on deposits and charging it on loans, some Islamic banks aim to enter into profit- and loss-sharing agreements with depositors and borrowers. But most are based on *murabaha* – another structure that bears a suspicious resemblance to an interest-bearing loan. In a *murabaha* contract, the provider of capital buys, say, a piece of machinery for $1,000, and the borrower buys it back from the bank later for $1,100. According to the *murabaha* rules, the $100 represents a "mark-up", but it works much the same as interest in everything but name.

Forced devotion, *The Economist*, February 17th 2001

86 **(d) Somebody submitted a review of the Bible and signed it "God". Once Amazon had removed this, another review was posted which opined that the Bible "is not as good as the film"**

Given the anonymity afforded by the format, it was inevitable that someone would submit a review of the Bible signed "God". It was removed – God is presumed not to use e-mail – but another review quickly popped up to take its place. The Bible, it opines, is "not as good as the film". There is also nothing to stop writers giving their own books glowing notices. One writer, Lev Grossman, was so mortified by the bad reviews that readers gave his first novel ("infantile trash", "puerile pap") that he submitted several anonymous ones of his own ("hilarious", "fabulous") to redress the balance. His ruse succeeded until he wrote an article detailing his deception. The fake reviews were promptly removed.

Amateurs on Amazon, *The Economist*, August 28th 1999

QUESTIONS

87 Argentina has acquired a reputation for being unfriendly and unsupportive to its scientists. Part of the blame may lie with:

a   A football star, Diego Maradona, who attributed his drug addiction and collapse to the Argentinian national team's unscrupulous doctors

b   Enrique Caputo, a top physics researcher and Nobel prize contender who in 1986 was named as the "other man" in a divorce case between two popular Argentinian actors

c   The Brazil Ministry of Science and National Education, which has a large enough share of GDP to lure away top researchers from neighbouring Argentina

d   The economy minister, Domingo Cavallo, who declared in the mid-1990s that scientists could "go wash dishes"

88 American television, while retaining its popularity abroad, may be declining at home. For example:

a   The ratings for 2001's Super Bowl were lower than the average ratings for a regular-season NFL game five years ago

b   Since 1985, the average number of television hours watched by Americans under 18 has fallen by more than one-fifth

c   According to a poll in February 2001, viewers were more familiar with an Apple Computer commercial run only once in 1990 than with any commercial shown in 1999 or 2000

d   A poll taken in 2000 showed that, for the first time in eight years, more American ten-year-olds could identify Bill Clinton than any character from "The Simpsons"

ANSWERS

87 **(d) The economy minister, Domingo Cavallo, who declared in the mid-1990s that scientists could "go wash dishes"**

Despite producing three Nobel prizewinners in the past 50 years, Argentina spends little on science and technology – a mere 0.35% of GDP. (Nearby Brazil spends almost five times as much in real terms.) As a result, the number of local research posts has fallen by half. Argentina's government has only itself to blame. In the 1970s, under the military junta, even mathematics textbooks were censored; at that time scientific research was taken out of universities' control and placed in the hands of military officials. With his comments, Mr Cavallo was only continuing a long habit of government mistrust and contempt. The scientists of Argentina may be frustrated, but so far none of them is taking it out on movie stars' marriages.

Unloved boffins, *The Economist*, February 24th 2001

88 **(b) Since 1985, the average number of television hours watched by Americans under 18 has fallen by more than one-fifth**

Although TV's overall decline is still relatively small, young people – the market's future and one of its most attractive segments for advertisers – are turning away at an alarming pace. In part this is thanks to newfound competition from the Internet. Still, many of TV's present woes are simply the perils of a cyclical industry. The year 2000 was unsustainably good, with a fortunate convergence of temporary business boosters, profligate dotcoms and an economic boom. It was an Olympic year, and also had a presidential election that went on and on, providing a surge in viewership for the news networks similar to that in wars. And a new show format – reality-based programming, such as "Survivor" – became a viewing obsession. After that, anything was bound to be a disappointment.

Television takes a tumble, *The Economist*, January 20th 2001

QUESTIONS

89 Why did the Russian Orthodox Church make a fuss about the computerisation of Russia's tax system?

a   The new system is likely to turn up an undeclared $350m salted away by the church
b   Some priests argued that the software used to calculate tax bills is "too Jewish"
c   The new bar codes used on tax forms resemble the binary code for the number six, apparently marking the forms with the devilish "number of the Beast", 666
d   The electronic tax forms list "Imam" as an occupation

90 If you were to speak of "the British solution" in Ireland, what would you probably be referring to?

a   The widespread theory that the potato famine of 1859–60 was engineered to reduce the Irish population
b   The success of schools in Northern Ireland, which some Irish politicians believe should be emulated in the Republic
c   Monarchy
d   Irish women travelling to England for legal abortions, which are banned at home

ANSWERS

89 (c) **The new bar codes used on tax forms resemble the binary code for the number six, apparently marking the forms with the devilish "number of the Beast", 666**

In early 2001, the Russian tax inspectorate introduced new tax forms to be read by computers. The three bar codes that appear at the beginning, middle and end of the tax forms each contain the binary code that represents the number six. 666 is best known in Christian theology as the "Number of the Beast", described in the Book of Revelations, which will mark the doomed as the apocalypse approaches. Thousands of taxpayers, thinking taxes bad enough without the additional threat of hellfire, refused to use the new forms. A theological commission set up by the Russian Orthodox Church announced it had found nothing sinister in the visual fluke and sternly warned the devout to go ahead and pay their taxes.

Tax beast, *The Economist*, March 3rd 2001

90 (d) **Irish women travelling to England for abortions, which are banned at home**

Although Ireland has relaxed its position on other touchy social issues, such as divorce and homosexuality, it remains the only western country, bar Malta, where abortion is virtually banned. The current regime, which affirms the right of Irish women to undergo the procedure in England but virtually outlaws it in Ireland, reflects the confused state of public opinion. The issue last boiled over in 1992, when Ireland's Supreme Court, considering the tragic case of a sexually abused teenager, ruled that suicidal tendencies could be grounds for abortion. A three-part ballot later tried but failed to clear up the legal mess, when voters agreed merely to uphold the right of women to receive information about abortion and to travel abroad to obtain it.

Ireland's sad and confusing secret, *The Economist*, December 9th 2000

QUESTIONS

91 **According to William Carlos Williams, the late American poet and paediatrician, what is a "variable foot"?**

a A haphazard unit of measurement used in New Jersey, his home state
b A metrical device with which he aimed to overthrow the poetical hegemony of iambic pentameter
c A side-effect of polio, which he found in some of his patients
d A euphemism for being a bad dancer

92 **How many commercial messages is the average American exposed to in a single day, according to industry experts?**

a 50
b 150 (of which 140 are ignored)
c 500 (of which 200 are ignored)
d 1,500

ANSWERS

91 (b) A metrical device with which he aimed to overthrow the poetical hegemony of iambic pentameter

What American poetry needed, Williams argued, was an authentic, modern and distinctively American voice. It should speak as people spoke, simply, idiomatically. Form as well as language had to be overhauled, the tyranny of the iambic pentameter overthrown, and to this end Williams developed a metrical device he called the "variable foot". "The rhythmic unit decided the form of my poetry," he later explained. "When I came to the end of a rhythmic unit (not necessarily a sentence) I ended the line." Old ways with grammar and typography were also rejected. Williams used lower-case letters at the beginning of lines, and punctuation marks quite sparingly.

Word as image, *The Economist*, March 3rd 2001

92 (d) 1,500

With Americans bombarded by 1,500 commercial messages daily, brands are screaming ever louder to be noticed above the noise. Take Pizza Hut, which helped to bankroll Russia's space agency by putting a ten-metre-high, $1.25m ad on a Proton booster rocket. Or the convoy of 20 car wrecks that crawled through Manhattan and Los Angeles promoting a car-chase video game. Marketing gimmicks are hardly new, but they are becoming more frequent, more extreme and more ubiquitous – earning a hip label all of their own: guerrilla marketing. Buzz matters more to brands now than ever before. If advertisers are smart, guerrilla marketing could evolve into something that is as focused as it is fun. If not, it will do little but add to the noise.

Guerrillas in our midst, *The Economist*, October 14th 2000

QUESTIONS

93 Who is reported to have said in 1989, "Those bloody bastards! ... We've got to do it or the common people will rebel!"?

a   An anonymous East German officer watching his men help take down the Berlin Wall
b   Subcomandante Marcos, deciding to found the movement that would eventually become the Zapatistas
c   An old hand in the Chinese Communist Party, Wang Zhen, supporting the use of force against protesters in Tiananmen Square
d   The writer Kingsley Amis to his son, Martin, describing the warm public reaction to rumours of a possible collaboration between them

94 Although Vietnam's first official stockmarket index has performed well – between July 2000 and March 2001, it rose 160% – western investors may find Vietnamese investing an unusual experience, because:

a   Computers are banned from the exchange, in case they are used to spread anti-government propaganda
b   The trading floor is open only three days a week, for an hour each day
c   Investors with government ties, or those who have paid massive bribes, are allowed to start trading an hour before anyone else
d   Some of the companies traded do not exist

ANSWERS

93 **(c) An old hand in the Chinese Communist Party, Wang Zhen, supporting the use of force against protesters in Tiananmen Square**

Despite the quotation, others likewise revealed in the important book "The Tiananmen Papers" strongly suggest that most of the standing committee of the Politburo, China's formal apex of power, were not hardliners who saw in the protests the germs of anarchy or, worse, another cultural revolution. The majority were reformers, led by Zhao Ziyang, then secretary-general of the Communist Party, who sought a dialogue with the students and was even ready to discuss their demands for a freer press, greater accountability for officials and a public reappraisal of the protests. Yet when consensus within the committee proved impossible, the hardliners, led by Li Peng, then prime minister, forced the issue by appealing to the surviving elders from the "first generation" of Communist revolutionaries.

China's lost decade, *The Economist*, March 3rd 2001

94 **(b) The trading floor is open only three days a week, for an hour each day**

The slowdown helped generate an insatiable demand for shares. Before each trading session opens, clients draw numbers from a hat, to determine the order in which their trades will be executed (with an upper limit of 10,000 shares a trade). After placing their orders, the hopefuls then sit patiently in the lounge, quietly discussing the movements on the electronic board, and occasionally drawing charts for each other on graph paper. A pleasant hour later, the exchange lets the broker know whose orders have been executed, and an employee calls out the lucky numbers to the group. Most would-be punters file out slowly. A few stay to collect their winnings. That, for now, is capitalism with Vietnamese characteristics.

Soaring Saigon, *The Economist*, March 17th 2001

QUESTIONS

95 The Chinese word for mobile phones is *dageda*, which literally means "big brother bigs". Why?

a   Because first-born sons, traditionally more prized in Chinese society, are more likely to receive mobile phones as gifts than their younger sisters
b   Because when mobile phones first appeared, only the highest-ranking government officials were allowed to own them
c   Because until recently only members of triad gangs, nicknamed "big brothers", could afford them
d   To contrast them with standard phones, often called "little brothers" because they are frequently used to talk to family and friends back home in smaller towns

96 Britain's Manchester United has more fans and bigger revenues than any other soccer team. Which of the following is true?

a   Merchandising and sponsors bring in over half of the club's revenues
b   The team has won the Premier League seven times in eight years
c   Manchester United's share price fell sharply in 2000
d   A quarter of the team's players have been to business school

ANSWERS

95 (c) Because until recently only members of triad gangs, nicknamed "big brothers," could afford them

A decade ago, China's phone system was awful, with one fixed line for every 100 people, and no mobile phones at all. Today, China has five times as many fixed lines as India, and 25 times as many mobile subscribers. Indeed, it is the mobile market where investors see the biggest pots of gold. The Chinese call mobile phones *dageda*, or "big brother bigs", because until recently only members of triad gangs (big brothers) could afford them. By the end of 2000, some 70m Chinese had become big brothers. By 2005 the number of subscribers could reach 240m, making China the largest mobile-phone market in the world.

The minister of arbitrary power, *The Economist*, December 9th 2000

96 (c) Manchester United's share price fell sharply in 2000

United has almost 14m fans across Europe, more than any other club. In Britain, it has nearly two-and-a-half times the number of supporters as Chelsea, the Premier League team with the next-largest fan base. But things are not quite as rosy as all that. United's share price has almost halved since the end of the 2000 season and 2000's pre-tax profits were 25% lower than 1999's at £16.8m, although television income increased by £8m. That was partly because United played five fewer home games, but the main culprit was what the outgoing chairman of Tottenham Hotspur, Alan Sugar, bitterly calls the "prune-juice effect" – as fast as money goes in, it comes out the other side in the form of players' wages.

It's a funny old game, *The Economist*, February 10th 2001

QUESTIONS

97 **All of the following were findings of *The Economist*'s 2001 Big Mac index, except one. Which is the exception?**

a   The yen is 14% overvalued against the euro, which should cheese off Japanese bankers

b   The dollar has never looked so overvalued during 15 years of burgernomics

c   The cheapest Big Macs are found in China, Malaysia, the Philippines and South Africa. Hence these countries have the most undervalued currencies

d   Australian and New Zealand dollars, which are both 40–45% below McParity, need to ketchup

98 **The philosophy of Immanuel Kant awed his contemporaries so much that he was dubbed**

a   *der Flammenwerfer*, "the flamethrower"

b   *der Alleszermalmer*, "the all-crusher"

c   *der Teppichfresser,* "the devourer of carpets"

d   *der Gottesmörder,* "the murderer of God"

ANSWERS

97 (a) **The yen is 14% overvalued against the euro, which should cheese off Japanese bankers**

Burgernomics is based upon one of the oldest concepts in international economics: the theory of purchasing-power parity (PPP). The Big Mac PPP is the exchange rate that would leave hamburgers costing the same in each country. Some of our readers find the Big Mac index hard to swallow. Not only does the theory of purchasing-power parity hold only for the very long run, but hamburgers are a flawed measure of PPP. Local prices may be distorted by trade barriers on beef, sales taxes, or big differences in the cost of property rents. Of course, the index was never intended to be a precise predictor of currency movements. It is simply a way to make exchange-rate theory a bit more digestible.

Big Mac currencies, *The Economist*, April 21st 2001

98 (b) *der Alleszermalmer*, "the all-crusher"

Kant sought to reconcile two dominant but conflicting traditions: the rationalism of Descartes and the sceptical empiricism of Hume. The result, if true, was to throw humanity back on its own cognitive resources. God, the soul and immortality became mere hypotheses; things in themselves were inaccessible to human perception; and certainty was possible only within the limits dictated by the apparatus of human thought. The entire structure of metaphysics and theology seemed to totter under the rigour of Kantian criticism. Even though his intention had not been to subvert religion or the state, he was dubbed *der Alleszermalmer*, the "all-crusher". Yet the instrument of his critical philosophy was not the blunt hammer of a Nordic god, but the clarifying precision of systematic thought.

Meet Mr Green, *The Economist*, May 5th 2001

QUESTIONS

99 Geri Halliwell, formerly known as Ginger Spice, endorsed Britain's Labour Party in the 2001 election. But how did she describe Tony Blair in 1997?

a "Completely unsnoggable"
b "Just not a safe pair of hands with the economy"
c "Weak on globalisation, and weak on the causes of globalisation"
d "The love child of a Communist and a North Pole elf"

100 Which musical hothouse spawned a rival in the Metropolitan Opera House Company in New York in the mid-1800s, and why?

a The Rockefellers' private music salon, because its audiences were overflowing on to Fifth Avenue and becoming drunk and disorderly
b The New York Academy of Music, because its 18 private boxes were monopolised by an old elite of Roosevelts and Stuyvesants, preventing access to other 19th-century millionaires
c Mrs Stuyvesant Fish's lavish teas for her friends' dogs, where the finest musicians and composers would show off their talents, because the barking obliterated the baritones
d Carnegie Hall, because Andrew Carnegie, a Pittsburgh steel man, had a staunch dislike for old money and barred the Manhattan elite from his concert hall

ANSWERS

99 (b) "Just not a safe pair of hands with the economy"

In the first big celebrity endorsement of the 2001 campaign, Geri Halliwell, a former Spice Girl, appeared in a Labour advert, serving tea to pensioners. (Britney Spears also declared for Labour.) Ms Halliwell's political opinions have evolved since 1997; then in her Thatcherite phase, she said that Tony Blair's hair was all right, but "he's just not a safe pair of hands with the economy". This could be due to the influence of Matthew Freud, Ms Halliwell's PR adviser, who is said to control not only what parties she attends, but also – possibly, since he is a friend of a former Cabinet member, Peter Mandelson – which ones she endorses.

On the trail, *The Economist*, May 17th 2001

100 (b) The New York Academy of Music, because its 18 private boxes were monopolised by an old elite of Roosevelts and Stuyvesants, preventing access to other 19th-century millionaires

Class struggle in late 19th-century New York between old and new money was fought on many terrains, but none so fiercely as grand opera. Most arrivistes reluctantly put up with the old elite's monopoly on the boxes. But William Vanderbilt, a rail-and-shipping magnate's son, refused to settle for a seat in the stalls: he bid $30,000 for a box – and was rebuffed. In riposte, he and other parvenus, including Goulds, Whitneys, Rockefellers and Morgans, contributed $10,000 each to incorporate a new opera boasting 122 private boxes, the Metropolitan Opera House Company. Soon old money had no choice but to join the Met, and differences were quickly forgotten as the two foes found common cause in keeping out the next generation of newcomers.

That other gilded age, *The Economist*, June 2nd 2001

101 Caribbean stock exchanges operate on a small scale. For example:

a There are just five companies listed on Trinidad's exchange, and one of them owns another
b Barbados had at least two working days in 2001 with no trades at all
c The market capitalisation of all existing Caribbean exchanges is less than Tiger Woods earned in 2000
d To boost revenues, Guyana's exchange has invested in a tourist restaurant/café where visitors can watch the trading

102 Why is the glassy-winged sharpshooter the bane of Californian vintners?

a It feasts exclusively and with a passion on the best grapes
b It pesters grape harvesters with its buzzing and stinging
c It transmits bacteria into the water vessels of plants
d She shoots vineyard workers from a helicopter

ANSWERS

101 (b) Barbados had at least two working days in 2001 with no trades at all

Barbados hardly looks unusual against a Caribbean backdrop better known for bananas and beaches than for high finance. In Trinidad, trading volume fell from 12% of market capitalisation in 1995 to 3% in 2000. The first Caribbean stock exchanges were set up when post-independence politicians dreamed of self-contained island economies. Foreign investment was barely tolerated, and exchange controls blocked the outward flow of home-grown savings. But many islands have since abolished or weakened exchange controls. Cable TV and the Internet encourage wealthier citizens to invest in New York. On the local markets, new listings are rare.

Island-hopping, *The Economist*, June 2nd 2001

102 (c) It transmits bacteria into the water vessels of plants

The glassy-winged sharpshooter, a native of the south-eastern United States that was first spotted in California in 1990, is an eclectic eater that can consume ten times its own weight in an hour. But the problem is not what it takes when it eats, but what it leaves behind. The sharpshooter is a very effective transmitter of a bacterium, *Xylella fastidiosa*, that blocks the water vessels in plants, eventually killing them. The bacterium affects numerous species, including many that thrive on California's farms, causing diseases such as almond leaf scorch, phoney peach disease, alfalfa dwarf, and oleander leaf scorch. Its most lethal impact, however, is on vines, where it causes Pierce's disease.

Grapeshot, *The Economist*, March 17th 2001

103 Which of these human traits is shown by the Kentish plover, a small bird?

a It sometimes gets divorced, abandoning its mate and offspring
b Males typically interrupt females with their singing
c Young birds are rebellious in adolescence before carefully copying parental behaviour in adulthood
d Female birds spend longer preparing to leave the nest than males

104 He has been convicted for heroin trafficking and accused of murder, but Mustafa Bayram (aka "Mustafa the Lame") stood to lose his parliamentary immunity in Turkey for:

a Defaming the name of Mustafa Kemal Ataturk (a jailable offence)
b Possessing an illegally enormous amount of Bulgarian tobacco and Iranian cloves
c Being married to seven women, four of whom did not know about the others
d Attempting to sell two stolen paintings by Picasso

ANSWERS

103 (a) **It sometimes gets divorced, abandoning its mate and offspring**
When Cole Porter wrote about birds, bees and educated fleas, he neglected to mention that, besides falling in love, animals also get divorced. In the case of plovers it is, more often than not, the female who abandons her mate and offspring. The most likely reason for this is that male plovers outnumber females. And since a lone parent does almost as well at raising chicks as both do together, there is little genetic cost to the parent that deserts first. Little, but not none. So it is worth leaving only if you can find a second mate, and then raise a second brood. Whether a bird deserts or stays depends on how it rates its chances elsewhere.

Seven-year twitch, *The Economist*, March 31st 2001

104 (d) **Attempting to sell two stolen paintings by Picasso**
The suddenly high-minded Turkish parliament acted after Mr Bayram, twice elected to the parliament by his clan's 40,000 votes, had been accused of trying to sell in Istanbul two stolen Picasso paintings, "The Clown" and one of a naked woman, using his chauffeur as a middleman. The paintings were among seven believed to have been taken from the Kuwaiti royal family by Iraqi troops during their invasion of the emirate in 1990, and smuggled into Turkey by Iraqi Kurds. Nicknamed "Mustafa the Lame" after being wounded in a 1991 shoot-out in which he allegedly killed two men, Mr Bayram ended up facing trial on two more recent charges of heroin trafficking, not to mention a murder case.

A Turkish lover of Picassos, *The Economist*, March 31st 2001

QUESTIONS

105 **Who declared himself "the best leader in the world" and hates being heckled, questioned or interrupted except by cheers?**

a   Leonid Kuchma (Ukraine)
b   Robert Mugabe (Zimbabwe)
c   Silvio Berlusconi (Italy)
d   Jiang Zemin (China)

106 **According to a leaked cable about a meeting in March 2001 between American and German officials, how did the US secretary of state, Colin Powell, describe Yasser Arafat?**

a   As having "lost touch with reality"
b   As "stupid, corrupt, and hopelessly stubborn"
c   As "the only person in the Middle East at all interested in peace"
d   As "lying to us with every word, right down to the way he folds his headscarf"

ANSWERS

105 (c) Silvio Berlusconi (Italy)

Small, bronzed and balding, Silvio Berlusconi oozes ambition and chutzpah, fancying himself as a kind of entrepreneurial, modern-day Napoleon, cutting a swathe across Europe. Some Italians think he is an angel persecuted by left-wing magistrates, unfairly despised by the political establishment, cold-shouldered by a snooty liberal intelligentsia. Others label him a crook who was lucky to survive the expulsion of his old-guard political sponsors from public life, whose first fortune was shadily acquired, and whose good luck in politics stems largely from his ownership of half of Italy's television channels and to the sparkling image that has afforded him. On one matter the two sides agree. His ego is as big as ever.

Silvio Berlusconi, Italy's would-be Napoleon, *The Economist*, March 24th 2001

106 (a) As having "lost touch with reality"

How and why did the cable get to the media? After reaching the foreign ministry, it was sent by the German ambassador to a top diplomatic adviser in the chancellery for editing and approval – and then given one of the lowest security classifications, "confidential: for internal use only", and circulated widely within the bureaucracy. And so, inevitably, outside it. Mr Powell's was not the only comment to cause a diplomatic stir. According to the leaked report, a top German official, recounting talks earlier in the month with Colonel Qaddafi, said that the Libyan leader had "admitted that Libya took part in terrorist actions ... He clarified that he had abandoned terrorism and seeks the opportunity to make Libya's new position known."

Plain speaking, plain cover-up, *The Economist*, May 26th 2001

QUESTIONS

107 Who said "The simmering magma is about to explode", and why?

a   Mark Cuban, a dotcom billionaire, on learning that his bid for the Dallas Mavericks basketball team had been accepted by Ross Perot Jr
b   Pierce Brosnan, in "Dante's Peak", a 1997 film about a volcano
c   George Bush, on hearing that an American spy plane had fallen into Chinese hands
d   Junichiro Koizumi, in a fit of flowery rhetoric after becoming Japan's new prime minister

108 A total of $11m was paid for 31 pieces on display by Damien Hirst at the Gagosian Gallery in New York in September 2000. What was the title of the work that first made him a star?

a   "Monet's Lisa"
b   "I Want to Spend the Rest of my Life Everywhere, with Everyone, One to One, Always, Forever, Now"
c   "The Physical Impossibility of Death in the Mind of Someone Living"
d   "Bisected Jersey Cow in the Mood for Love"

ANSWERS

107 (d) **Junichiro Koizumi, in a fit of flowery rhetoric after becoming Japan's new prime minister**

Mr Koizumi will now have to prove that he is more than a "poster boy for the elections", as Naoto Kan, a leading opposition politician, is calling him. With his shaggy permed hair and outspoken views, Mr Koizumi's carefully cultivated image as a political eccentric made him popular with voters, who are heartily sick of mainstream politics, though, as the LDP's election has shown, Mr Koizumi can play factional politics with as much finesse as any insider. If truth be told, Mr Koizumi is closer to elements within the main opposition Democratic Party of Japan than he is to much of his own party. A fundamental realignment of Japanese politics, long predicted and long overdue, may beckon again.

A magician in Japan, *The Economist*, April 28th 2001

108 (c) **"The Physical Impossibility of Death in the Mind of Someone Living"**

Mr Hirst does not actually make anything much any more. Gone are the days when he sloshed around in a tank injecting a (dead) tiger shark with formaldehyde to create "The Physical Impossibility of Death in the Mind of Someone Living". The only piece at his recent show in New York to which Mr Hirst put a hand was an unfinished painting in a glass case called "Concentrating on Self Portrait as a Pharmacist". Still, demand for anything by Damien Hirst is so high that even copies of the invitation to the show (a pillbox designed by Mr Hirst containing details of the exhibition) have been sold on the eBay auction website.

Portrait of the artist as a brand, *The Economist*, February 10th 2001